Easy-to-Make
DECORATIVE KITES

Step-by-Step Instructions for 9 Models from Around the World

by Alan & Gill Bridgewater

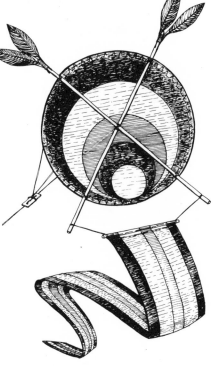

Dover Publications, Inc., New York

Contents

Published in Canada by General Publishing Company, Ltd., 30 Lesmill Road, Don Mills, Toronto, Ontario.

Published in the United Kingdom by Constable and Company, Ltd., 10 Orange Street, London WC2H 7EG.

Easy-to-Make Decorative Kites: Step-by-Step Instructions for 9 Models from Around the World is a new work, first published by Dover Publications, Inc., in 1985.

Manufactured in the United States of America
Dover Publications, Inc., 31 East 2nd Street, Mineola, N.Y. 11501

Library of Congress Cataloging in Publication Data

Bridgewater, Alan.
  Easy-to-make decorative kites.

  1. Kites. I. Bridgewater, Gill. II. Title.
TL759.B75 1985   629.133′32   85-12880
ISBN 0-486-24981-6 (pbk.)

1. Introduction

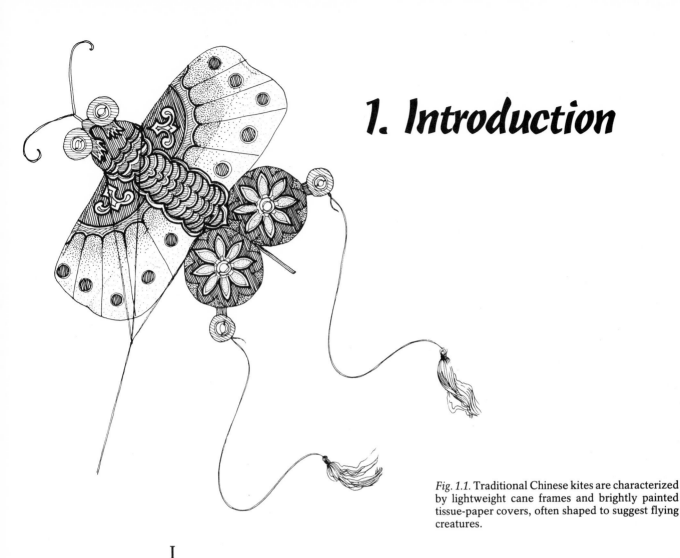

Fig. 1.1. Traditional Chinese kites are characterized by lightweight cane frames and brightly painted tissue-paper covers, often shaped to suggest flying creatures.

I

SOME PEOPLE, perhaps mindful of the old expression, "Go fly a kite," think that kite flying is pointless and a waste of time, or at best, like playing with marbles, suitable only for young children. We disagree, and history supports our view. For thousands of years, kites have played an important role in the social, military, economic, and religious life of the peoples of the Far East. When in the seventeenth century kites were introduced to Europe from China, Westerners acquired not just a new and exciting sport and leisure activity, but also a medium of scientific discovery. For over a century, kites have been instrumental in our understanding of aerodynamic laws and in the development of modern aircraft.

But beyond the excitement of participating in a historically distinguished activity, there is nothing quite like the thrill of creating your own kite and flying it—making one out of wood and paper, or fabric and plastic, watching it reach out into the sky, and seeing it swoop, hover, and glide in the infinite blue. These experiences—mind-soothing, even inspirational—are like no other and should not be missed.

In this book, we have made kite building and flying easy for you. The projects are fully illustrated and include step-by-step instructions, enabling even the beginner in a basic home workshop to make nine beautiful kites of various ethnic origins and ranging in sophistication from the simple, universally familiar diamond kite to the "high-tech" box kite. You won't need many tools, and the materials are few and inexpensive. We've included directions for decorating, rigging, and flying, as well as actually constructing, your kites, making this as complete a guide as we could.

II

More than half of the kites in this book are of Asiatic origin. This is fitting, since kites were being flown in China, Japan, and other eastern Asian countries centuries before they were introduced in the West. Over two thousand years ago, silk-and-bamboo kites were used in China for amusement, in religious celebrations, and for signaling and other military purposes. When paper was invented there, at the latest by about 100 B.C., kites became more widely available and were flown everywhere in festivals, in private celebrations, to bring good luck, by fishermen (to signal wind direction and sometimes even to bear the hooks), and as a competitive sport. Kite flying began in Japan some centuries later, but it quickly became as culturally important as in China.

Kite flying in Japan developed into a rich tradition. Elaborately decorated kites are still flown at New Year's celebrations and times of harvest, though these activities have been somewhat curtailed by urbanization. Even near cities, however, kites continue to be flown for amusement. Before World War II, the Japanese built a gigantic kite weighing over three-quarters of a ton, which was flown annually. Kite fighting is a popular sport in Japan, as elsewhere in the Orient. In a kite fight, combatants, using specially designed, easily maneuverable kites with lines bearing cutting and abrasive edges, try to disable one another's kites or actually cut the lines of their opponents' kites.

Similar kite-related traditions exist in many countries of the Far East and in countries with a large Asiatic immigrant population. A modified Malayan diamond kite is the classic model of many European and American kites. The kite-makers of Java, Indonesia, were once considered the most skillful in the world.

In the West—and Western-influenced countries like Australia—kites played a crucial role in scientific investigations, particularly in the development of modern aircraft. Benjamin Franklin's successful use of a kite in 1752 to demonstrate the identity of electricity and lightning is the most famous kite-related incident in the Western world. The nineteenth and early twentieth centuries saw a frenzy of experimentation, for scientific and military purposes, with kites and kite-derived aircraft. Large man-carrying gliders based on kite designs were built by many, including Sir George Cayley (called the "father of British aero-

nautics"), Captain B. F. S. Baden-Powell (brother of the founder of the Boy Scouts), Alexander Graham Bell (better known as the inventor of the telephone), the German inventor Otto Lilienthal (who had a significant influence on the Wright brothers), and the brothers Orville and Wilbur Wright themselves, whose successful powered flight in a heavier-than-air vehicle is history—and who had been expert kite fliers in their youth. Some of the finest early aerial photographs were taken from kites, and kites for some time served in many countries as instruments for gathering data for weather forecasts. As recently as 1931, kites were regularly sent aloft for this purpose by the U.S. Weather Bureau.

Many standard kite designs date back centuries, but one of the best known is a relatively recent invention: the box kite, invented by Lawrence Hargrave in Australia in 1893. This scientifically sophisticated kite has been invaluable in aerodynamic research, having led to the development of the wing design of the biplane. Yet the box kite has also become one of the most popular kites for recreational flying, and it is very commonly seen. You will learn to make one in Chapter 10.

Another important modern type of kite is the Eddy kite (named for its inventor, the American journalist William A. Eddy), invented in 1891. This kite, however, is not essentially different from a classic two-stick Malayan design (though even Hargrave's invention was not without an ancient Japanese precursor). It derives its flying efficiency and ability to lift heavy weights from the fact that its horizontal spar is *bowed* to a convex shape. Other even more unusual and original kite designs are a significant part of modern aerospace technology.

Fig. 1.2. An English Kite. This is a popular modification of the even more popular European Diamond Kite. Both of these traditional designs may be seen everywhere.

Fig. 1.3. In Japan, as in many Far Eastern countries, kite flying is a traditional cultural activity.

Fig. 1.4. In Guatemala the Indians welcome the sun and ancestral spirits by making and flying huge seven-stick kites.

III

Neither the most unusually shaped Chinese or Japanese kite nor even the efficient "high-tech" box kite is very hard to make. For most of the kites in this book, you will need only a few simple tools found around the house: a sharp knife, a pencil, a ruler (preferably a yardstick), a pair of scissors, and needles for sewing. For some projects it will help to have a sewing machine, and you will need a heavy needle with a large eye (sailmaker's needle or bodkin) for drawing tape through fabric. One project requires a pair of drawing compasses; another, a hand drill; for two projects, you will need a fine-tooth saw; and you may also need some colored felt-tip markers or brushes for applying inks.

As for material, some kites need more than others, but all require certain kinds of basic items.

You will need material for the *frame*, the skeleton of the

Fig. 1.5. In 1752, Benjamin Franklin (1706–1790), the great American printer, author, publisher, inventor, scientist, and statesman, used a simple cross-stick kite in his famous "electricity-catching" experiments.

kite (which includes the *spars*). This is frequently made of a type of cane, such as bamboo or rattan. Cane is used for the structure of most of the kites in this book, but you can make substitutions, using even wood from a packing crate. Kite frames may be made of any of a number of light, durable substances, including wood dowels, fiberglass, and aluminum tubing. Each of these latter materials is used for one kite project here.

Fig. 1.6. Samuel Franklin Cody (ca. 1861–1913) was a flamboyant American showman from the West (though unrelated to the more famous "Buffalo Bill" Cody) who as a naturalized British subject became official aeronautics advisor to the British government. He is seen here with his "bat" kite design. He developed several man-carrying kites and finally a huge airplane. He is credited with having made the first official powered airplane flight in England, on May 14, 1909 (he had managed some unofficial flying in October, 1908).

Another essential part of the kite is the *sail cover* (or *sail*, or *cover*). This is the material that is stretched over the frame. The sail cover is usually made of either a strong, light paper or a similarly strong, light fabric. This fabric may be of any type, from silk—the traditional Chinese sail-cover material—to a modern synthetic. Two kites in this book use clear plastic film for their sail covers.

You will also need string, preferably a fine cotton twine for lashing the *spars* (main frame members) together, a heavier cord for the *bridle* (*bridle lines*, *bridle legs*, or *harness*: the cords that link the kite frame to the flying line) and possibly for the *tail* (for which you may instead use ribbon or paper tape), and sturdy but lightweight cord for the flying line itself (nylon fishing line usually serves well). You will need a reel for winding the line (you can use a

Fig. 1.7. In Australia in 1893, Lawrence Hargrave (1850–1915) invented a kite of the square-cell or "box" type. His designs were used in the development of early biplanes.

Fig. 1.9. The American brothers Wilbur and Orville Wright (1867–1912; 1871–1948) started their now famous experiments in 1899, when they built and flew large kites. The glider shown here was flown in 1902.

fishing reel, or it can be a simple homemade affair of scrap wood); paper paste (homemade flour-and-water paste may be used); a tube of resin glue; a ring, rings, or plate (usually of metal) for bridle-point attachments, making an adjustable bridle, or using as a *tow ring* to join line and bridle; cotton tape; thread for tacking; and for some kites a few other easily obtainable items, such as inks for coloring.

When you are out flying your kite it is a good idea to be ready for anything, so carry a "kite kit": extra flying line, an extra tail (when appropriate), sticky tape, a knife, gloves, sunglasses, adhesive bandages, and a flight notebook and pencil.

And speaking of flying, each kite has its own flying characteristics, which we will discuss in the appropriate place; here we will provide a few general tips and cautions for novice kite flyers. Select a clear launch site, a wide-open space away from tall buildings, rivers, traffic, thorny shrubbery, and low-flying aircraft! Forest clearings and parks surrounded by high-rise buildings are less suitable than you might think—they create unstable wind conditions.

Never fly your kite in the rain. Last, but most important, *never fly your kite anywhere near overhead power lines!*

If you wear dark glasses, you will avoid worrying about the sun's hurting your eyes, and a pair of gloves will prevent friction burns. And, naturally, it will be futile to attempt to fly your kite if there is no wind!

Fig. 1.8. Around the turn of the century, Alexander Graham Bell (1847–1922), the inventor of the telephone, invented the tetrahedral kite, the basis for a series of huge man-carrying gliders and of innovations in aviation technology. In 1907, he founded the Aerial Experiment Association.

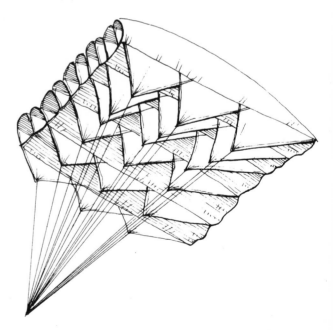

Fig. 1.10. A Parafoil, a kite and parachute sail of revolutionary design, was developed in the early 1950s by an American, Domina C. Jalbert.

IV

Finally, making all of the kites in this book requires the fastening, or *lashing* together, of joints, and similar basic operations. We have illustrated methods of lashing, as well as some useful ways of reinforcing your kite, here. Study the drawings, and refer back to them as necessary.

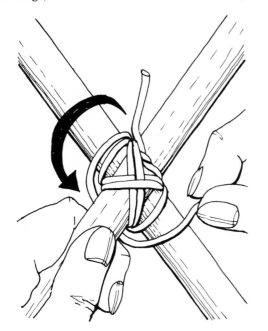

Fig. 1.11. Most traditional kites have a lashed central "X," or cross. Using damp cotton twine, lash the "X" as shown, pull the twine tight, and knot it. When the twine has dried, it will shrink and pull the crossed spars firmly together. Check to see that you have lashed the spars correctly and in the right place. When you are satisfied, dribble some resin glue over the lashing to keep it from coming loose.

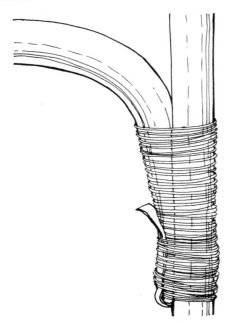

Fig. 1.12. Rattan can be bent and the joints lashed as shown. Notice how the "tail" of the shaped cane is tucked back. Finish off with a dribble of resin glue.

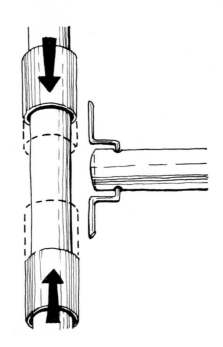

Fig. 1.13. A simple bent-wire-and-sliding-ring frame joint. The spar end is cut to fit snugly, and the rings are then slid over the wire ends.

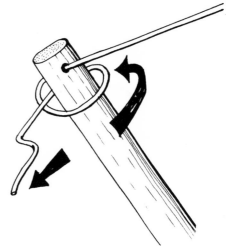

Fig. 1.14. One means of connecting the frame line to a spar end.

Fig. 1.15. To tighten the frame line, overbind as shown with a band of fine twine lashing.

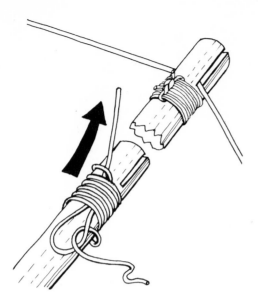

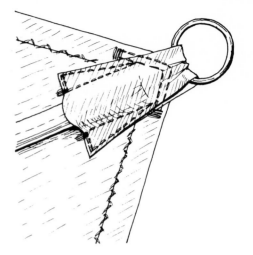

Fig. 1.16. (Upper right:) The finished connection of frame line to spar end (but using a *notch* instead of a hole). (Lower left:) Illustration of the knotting method.

Fig. 1.18. Attachment of a bridle-point ring (for tying on a bridle line) by means of a pocket of cloth sewn to the spar end and sail cover.

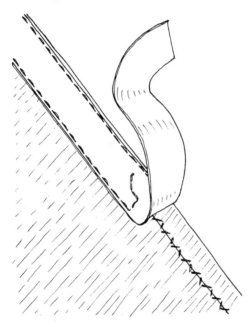

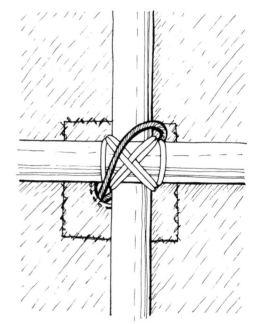

Fig. 1.17. For a really strong sail-cover edge, hem the fabric with a zigzag stitch, then sew on a tape strengthener.

Fig. 1.19. When a bridle or tow line is attached directly to crossed spars, as shown here, it is a good idea to reinforce the sail cover with an added thickness of fabric and a brass eyelet or oversewn hole.

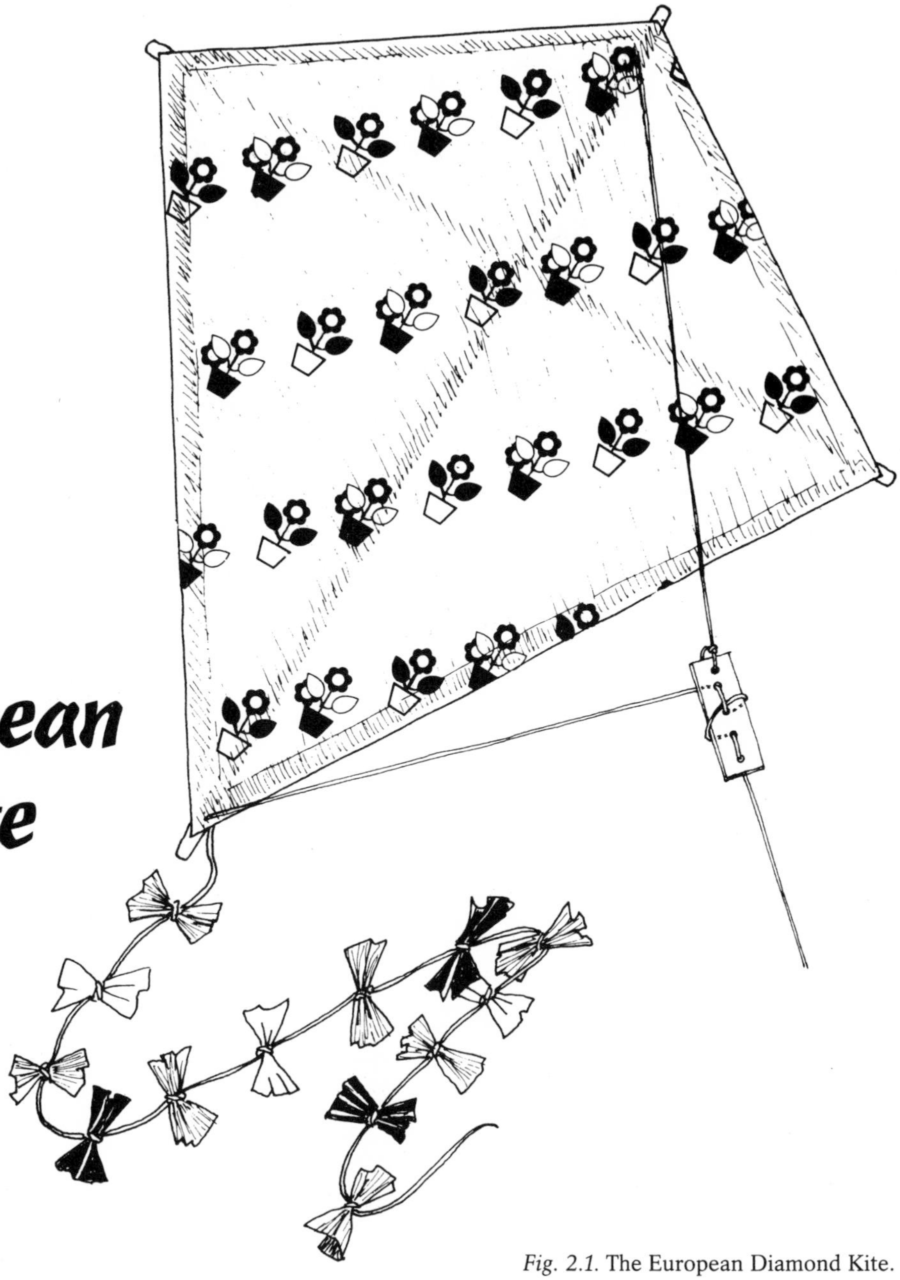

Fig. 2.1. The European Diamond Kite.

2. The European Diamond Kite

ASK A CHILD of about five or six to draw a kite, and he will draw a diamond kite. This kite originated in Asia as a Malay two-stick, but so long ago did it become the classic kite in Europe and America that its very shape is now synonymous with the word "kite."

The familiar European Diamond is an ideal starter kite for beginners and children: it is easy to make, and once made tends to perform well. The lashed central "X" joint is straightforward and the spar-end frame lines almost self-tensioning. There are no complex measurements or difficult-to-obtain materials.

We've chosen to make our European Diamond Kite of gift-wrapping paper and split bamboo, but there's no reason why you can't substitute, say, brown paper and wood dowels; cotton fabric and fiberglass rods; sheets of plastic and metal tubes; or even, in a pinch, newspaper and split packing-case wood. For the most part you can still use the directions we have given, automatically making the substitutions along the way. Just be sure you choose a lightweight material for the sail cover and a straight and strong material for the spars. This classic kite is best flown with a two-leg bridle and slip-plate or ring tow point (see Fig. 2.1). To make the kite as pictured here, you will need a sheet of gift-wrapping paper at least 36″ × 36″, a straight length of bamboo cane about 36″ long and ¾″ thick, fine cotton twine, enough paper and string for the tail, and some of the other basic tools and materials we mentioned in the previous chapter. When purchasing the bamboo, avoid canes that are green or dark brown; also they should not sound shattered when you tap them on the ground.

Making the Frame

When making the frame, keep in mind that it needs to be as light as possible and well balanced. Take the 36″ length of cane and, with your sharp, heavy knife, split it down its length. Follow the grain and use a twisting motion (see Fig. 2.2). (You may have trouble at the nodes; go slowly, with a seesawing motion. You may find it necessary to tap your knife blade carefully with a mallet.) Try to achieve half-canes that are, as far as possible, evenly split, smooth-edged, and free of splinters, cracks, and weak areas. Use sandpaper to eliminate rough edges, especially around the nodes. Then cut the pieces to length, place them so that cut side faces cut side (Fig. 2.3), and position them on your work surface so that the horizontal cane crosses the vertical cane 12″ from the top (the rule is one-third down the length of the vertical spar; see Fig. 2.4). Take enough cotton twine to bind the spars, dampen it slightly, and lash the "X" so that it is firm and fixed at a 90° angle. Make sure that the form and strength of the frame are exactly as you want them, wait for the twine to dry, and finally dribble some resin glue over the bound joint to make sure it stays put (see Fig. 2.5).

Now rig up the frame line. Place the kite frame squarely

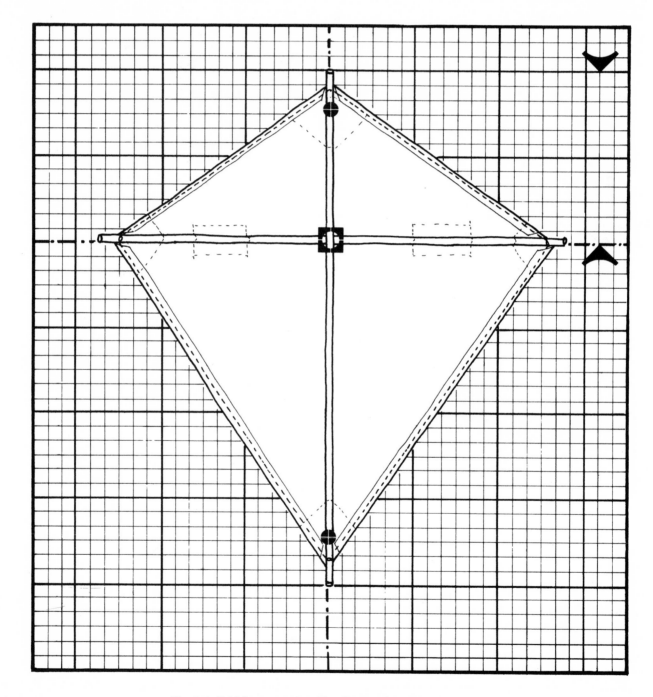

Fig. 2.4. Grid for measuring. The distance between the arrows represents one foot (each small square stands for a square inch).

on your work surface, and, starting at the tail (bottom) end, knot the frame line (Fig. 2.6), run it up to near one end of the horizontal spar, and, holding it taut, knot it at that point. Now bring it up to the next spar end, knot again, and so on, tying it fast at the bottom where you started. (To make your frame line more secure, drill holes in the spar

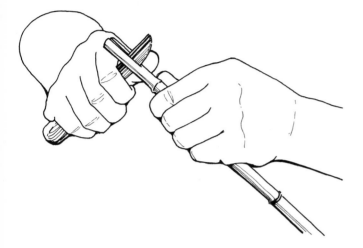

Fig. 2.2. Splitting bamboo is no problem as long as the knife is sharp and you work with a controlled knife-twisting action.

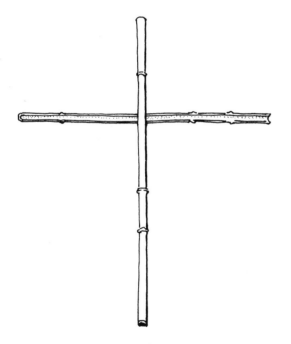

Fig. 2.3. Positioning the split canes.

ends and tie as shown in Figs. 1.14 and 1.15.) When you are satisfied that the classic diamond shape is well balanced and the frame lines are taut and evenly tensioned, dribble some resin glue over all knots and twine ends.

NOTE: In kite making, precise measurements are less important than balance, proportion, and symmetry. For example, for this kite you can use a horizontal cane that measures only 32". The "wing" sides, however, should be well balanced. That is, you should position the horizontal

spar on the vertical spar so that the former is divided in half (by *weight*) as precisely as possible. Any care you take at this stage of construction will be repaid many times over when you attempt to fly your kite. You will have an unpleasant time trying to get an unbalanced kite to fly properly!

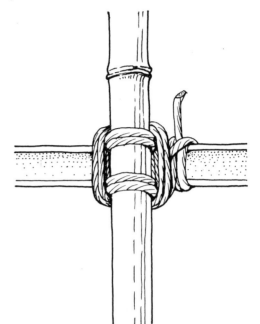

Fig. 2.5. Lashing the "X."

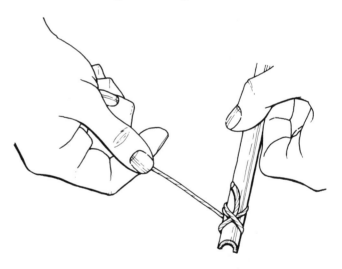

Fig. 2.6. Knotting the line.

Attaching the Sail Cover

Now you will need your pencil, scissors, and paper paste, as well as the sheet of gift-wrapping paper. Spread the paper face-down on your work surface. Place the kite frame over the paper (make sure you have waited till all the glue has dried!), and draw around it to duplicate the shape of the kite, except that you must *add a 1" margin where the lines are*. Now dampen the margin area and cover it with paste.

Wait a few minutes for the paste to soak in, meanwhile positioning the frame exactly where you want it. Now turn the paste-covered margin over the frame line and press it down securely, working along until the paper is secured over the line (Fig. 2.7). Take some extra strips of the wrapping paper, cover with paste, and use them to "bridge" the spars, reinforcing areas subject to stress (Fig. 2.8; see also Fig. 2.4). Smooth them neatly in place. Then let all the paste dry. You will notice that, as the sail cover begins to dry, it will shrink so that the frame line will be slightly pulled in and tightened. This is as it should be.

Finally, when all is dry, give the whole kite a couple of coats of varnish, paper glaze, or similar medium. This will help to strengthen the kite, making it resistant to rain, puddles, ponds, and the like.

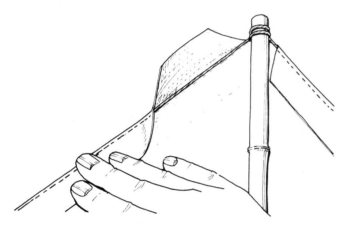

Fig. 2.7. Make sure that the pasted-down paper is smooth and free from wrinkles.

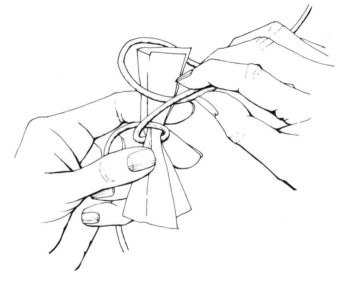

Fig. 2.8. Reinforcing the spars.

Making the Tail

For a kite of this size and character, the tail needs to be about 20 feet long. If you are eager to get your kite into the sky you can simply use a plastic ribbon or maybe a crepe-paper streamer. We've chosen to make a traditional tail of twisted paper bows and string. Make about 60 twisted paper bows (three bows to the foot) and tie them into the string with loop or running knots (Fig. 2.9). You can simply tie the tail onto the bottom of the kite's spine, or you can make a little toggle-and-loop fastener.

The Bridle

We've seen diamond kites with any of a number of bridle points: head, tail, and wingtips; head, tail, cross point, and wingtips; etc. There are many variations and combinations. We've given this kite, however, two bridle points: one at the head and one at the tail (see dark circles in Fig. 2.4). Use about 5′ of a smooth cotton cord for the bridle. Place the kite on the work surface, spar side down. Carefully pierce the paper sail cover, pass the bridle ends through the cover, and fasten them to the spar with knots. You can now attach the flying line to the bridle with a ring, a sliding metal plate, a wooden toggle, or even a sliding knot. (Another method is to make one bridle leg a continuation of the flying line; see Fig. 2.1.) It is important for you to be able to adjust this tow point to suit changing wind conditions. For example, if the wind is a bit stiff, you can slide the tow ring along the bridle so that it is nearer the kite head. This allows the kite's tail to rise—perfect for high-wind conditions!

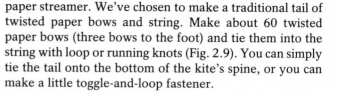

Fig. 2.9. The knot being used here is a clove hitch.

Flying Line and Reel

For a lightweight, relatively low-flying kite of this shape and size, ordinary nylon fishing line makes a perfectly good flying line. Buy two or three hundred yards for starters; you can always add more if the kite performs well. You will need a reel to keep the line from getting tangled. If you are a beginner and just can't wait to launch your kite, you can improvise a reel quickly from a smooth-edged can or cardboard food canister. But we particularly recommend making a flat plywood "slip reel" (use Fig. 2.10 as a pattern; see also Fig. 2.11). It is simple to make, easy to use, and allows for swift line runoff.

Flying the European Diamond Kite

Follow the general tips on kite flying given in the previous chapter. In a steady, moderate wind, this kite should almost leap out of your arms. If, even after a short run, the kite fails to rise, or if it rises but then bucks or falters in flight, try adjusting the tow point and/or altering the tail length (remember to carry an additional length of tail with you). It is a good idea to keep notes of wind conditions and any adjustments you have made. Gradually you will build up a body of information that will help you fly your kites more efficiently, and when you construct your next kite, you may be able to make advantageous design changes.

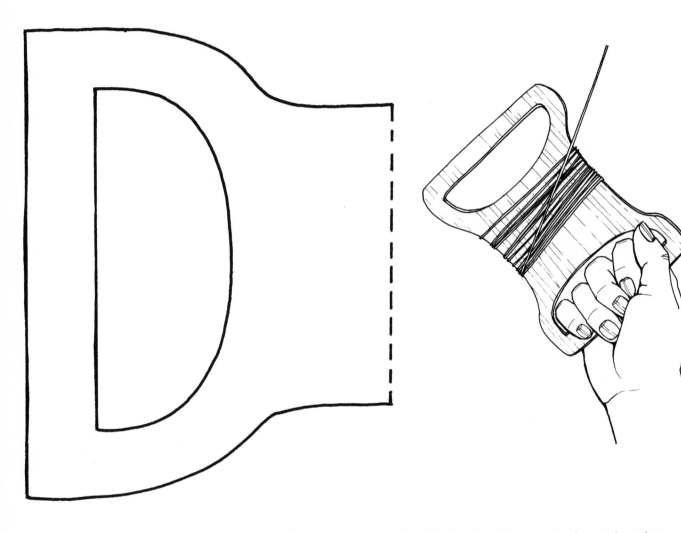

Fig. 2.10. Pattern for the plywood "slip reel."

Fig. 2.11. Completed slip reel—simple to make and use.

3. The Japanese Red Devil Swooper Kite

Fig. 3.1. This brightly colored, highly maneuverable Japanese kite is best flown with dual bridles and flying lines. It uses tassel stabilizers instead of a tail.

THE JAPANESE RED DEVIL SWOOPER might almost be called the "International" kite: it looks a little like the traditional Indian Fighter; it has almost the proportions of the English bow-top kite and its arched top also resembles that of the French Pear Kite; and it performs rather like the Korean Fighter. This adds up to a good all-around swooper, ideal for kite fighting, fancy maneuvering, or just easy flying. Its ease in handling results from two special features: dual flying lines and a bowed, or arched, top spar. Shaping this spar is the only tricky aspect of making the Japanese Red Devil. On the whole the construction of this snappy kite is straightforward and uncomplicated and can be accomplished in no more than about three or four hours—a

little longer if you want to add an extra special touch or two.

You will need the usual tools and materials, plus two bamboo canes 36″ long and ¼″ thick, a 36″ × 36″ sheet—and a few scraps—of good wet-strength colored tissue paper (a kind suitably sturdy for a kite), a pair of rubber gloves, and a kettle for boiling water. Here is a bit of advice on buying the bamboo canes: take your time and be very choosy. Try to find, if possible, canes that are relatively even in thickness and free from obvious kinks, flaws, and weak areas. Of course, by its very nature, a bamboo cane tends to be thicker at one end. This can cause construction and balance problems, but just do your best. Adjustments for weight and balance can always be made later.

Making the Bowed Spar

Bamboo can be bent and shaped in a number of ways but we have found the soaking-and-kettle-steaming method to be the simplest and least hazardous. Inspect your two canes and decide which one will best stand up to a fair amount of handling. Soak it overnight in water. When you are ready to begin the shaping, put on the rubber gloves and have ready a ruler, some cotton twine, and the soaked cane. Boil water in the kettle and position the spout so you can hold and manipulate the cane in the flow of steam easily and without danger of accident. Check the measuring diagram (Fig. 3.2); you will see that the spar to be arched will be bent into a semicircle with a 28″ diameter, and this is what you should work toward.

Now hold the soaked bamboo cane over the steam, and begin to apply pressure gently (see Fig. 3.3). Once you have felt it give slightly, move your hands along the cane, and gently apply steam and pressure to another area. Do not try to force the cane into shape or it might snap. Gently work it until it begins to bend, and ease it into shape gradually, applying steam and working your hands up and down the length of cane repeatedly, exerting a slight pressure with your thumbs all the while. If an area is resistant, give it a good dose of steam and continue to work at it. Don't forget to wear the rubber gloves, and be careful not to knock over the kettle, set anything on fire, let the water boil out, or poke out an eye with the end of a cane. If you are reasonably cautious, steaming the bamboo into shape is not particularly dangerous. It is, however, an operation in the vicinity of which you should definitely not allow small children to play.

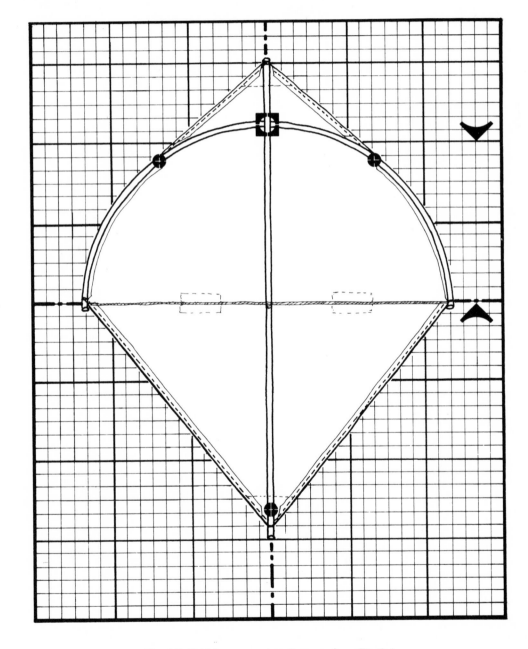

Fig. 3.2. Grid for measuring. Same scale as Fig. 2.4.

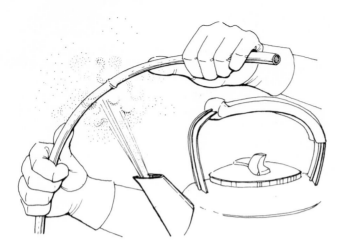

Fig. 3.3. Bending the cane.

When the cane has been bent into the desired shape (consult Fig. 3.2 and check with your ruler), connect the two ends with a length of twine; knot the twine securely to the spar ends and pull it taut (see Fig. 3.4). Allow the bent spar and twine to cool off and dry out.

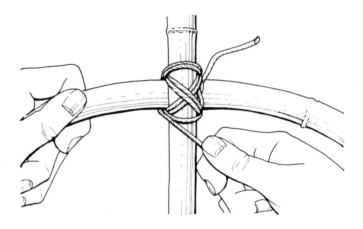

Fig. 3.4. Positioning the canes.

Assembling the Frame

Now place the straight piece of bamboo on your work surface with the thicker end nearer you; this will be the tail end. Take the bowed and strung spar and place it across the straight spar as in Fig. 3.4. The string should cross the vertical spar at its halfway point, causing the top of the bow

to be about 5″ below the top of the vertical spar. Also, the "wings" thus formed should be symmetrical. Make sure this is so before you lash the spars together. It always pays to take pains at this stage of construction; it will save you needless trouble later on, when you are attempting to get your kite into the air.

Lash the spars firmly together with dampened twine, making a tight "X" (Fig. 3.5). Also lash to the vertical spar the cord connecting the ends of the bowed spar. Before it is too late, test for balance by holding fingers at the ends of the vertical spar as shown in Fig. 3.6. The frame should lie straight and not tip to one side. Tighten the lashings and allow them to dry. If you find that the frame is unbalanced, you can make a correction later on by adding a counterbalance of extra tassels. But of course it is better to get it right at this stage.

Next, string frame lines from the bow tips to the tail and from the head to the bow arch (see Figs. 3.1 and 3.2 for placement). Knot them securely. When the entire frame has dried out, dribble resin glue over all lashings and knots.

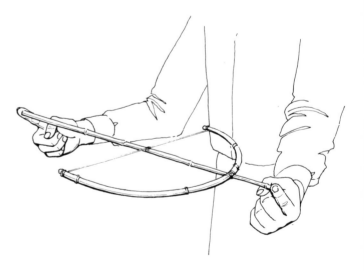

Fig. 3.5. Lashing the "X."

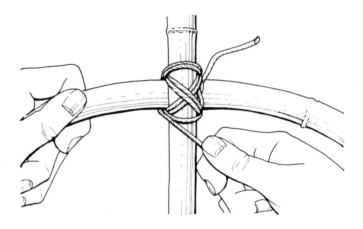

Fig. 3.6. Testing for balance.

Making the Sail Cover

Now dampen the square of tissue paper by placing it between two sheets of damp paper or by using an atomizer. Then gently compress the whole dampened sheet into a ball. Next, spread it out again and smooth it flat on your work surface. Place the kite frame over it and mark the paper for cutting, leaving an extra margin of 1″ between the frame lines and outer parts of the bowed spar, and the line along which you will cut the tissue paper. When you are sure that this has been done correctly, cut out the tissue paper. Knick "V" shapes into the margin where the paper will cover the bowed spar (see Fig. 3.1) so it can be fitted around the curves. Cover the margin surfaces with paste and smooth the edges down over the lines and spar ends, making sure the margin is crisply defined. Paste two strips of tissue paper over the bow string, fastening it to the wings of the sail cover (see Fig. 3.2). It is a good idea to reinforce with strips of scrap tissue paper all of the stress areas, too: head, tail, wingtips, and bridle points.

Decorating the Sail Cover

You can decorate this kite with ink or paint (just be sure to avoid heavy buildup when using acrylics, and don't saturate the tissue paper), but there are advantages to decorating the sail cover by pasting down pieces of tissue paper of a different color. This is very easy to do, it looks good, and you can add additional layers to compensate for an imbalance of weight in the kite. When you paste on the pieces of tissue paper, smooth them gently in place; dab rather than rub, and watch out for color bleed. (See Fig. 3.7.) After you have decorated the sail cover and are satisfied that the kite has been well assembled, set it aside to dry thoroughly. Then, to strengthen it, give the whole thing a couple of coats of varnish or similar medium.

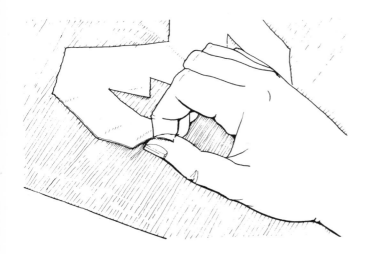

Fig. 3.7. Decorating the sail cover.

Wing Tassels

Wing tassels, besides being part of the decoration, help stabilize the kite. They are very simple to make: just double up bunches of thin strips of tissue paper, tie them in two places as shown in Fig. 3.8, and attach them to the wingtips. To make sure the kite is perfectly balanced, test again for balance (see Fig. 3.6). While you are holding the kite as illustrated, another person can add strips to or take them away from the tassels, or, for smaller adjustments, trim their ends with a pair of scissors.

Kites of this type are normally flown without a tail, but if after all adjustments you find that the kite tends to buck or stall in the air, a simple streamer tied to the tail end should add the drag that is necessary for stability.

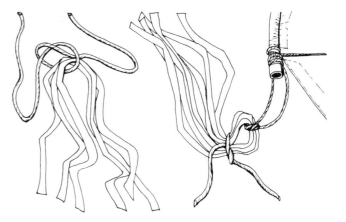

Fig. 3.8. Wing tassels.

The Bridle and Flying Lines

Although this kite can be flown with an ordinary single two-leg—head and tail—bridle, it will display its characteristically exceptional maneuverability only with *two* bridles and flying lines. To attach the bridles, place the kite, frame-side-down, on your work surface. Carefully pierce the sail at the two points along the bowed spar and the point at the tail that are indicated by crossed black circles in Fig. 3.2. Take two pieces of suitable cord, each about 5′ long, and tie them onto the spars (the two bottom legs come together at the tail end).

Since you will be steering and swooping the kite, it is important to have strong and smooth flying lines. Heavyweight nylon is excellent. Whatever kind of line you choose, be aware that if it is fluffy, it may just twist and bind. Attach the lines to the bridles using simple rings as tow points (see Fig. 3.1).

The Reels

For a kite that has two bridles and two lines, you will naturally need two reels, one for each hand. Two of the simple plywood slip type used in the last project (see Chapter 2, above) will be fine. A pattern for a slightly different type is given as Fig. 3.9. This one has a notched "rest" slit. You can make it easily from ¼" or ½" plywood; just measure, cut with a fretsaw, and rub down.

Flying the Japanese Red Devil Swooper Kite

The special fun of flying this kite is in being able to steer it through a series of stalls, swoops, and dives, using the two flying lines. It will take some practice: getting a kite of this type to perform a set of stunts is a skill that requires some concentration and a fair amount of eye, hand, and mind coordination. Be warned here that the kite is very sensitive to the controls, so at first just move your hands a little bit at a time, and slowly.

Launching this kite is a bit more complicated than launching an ordinary one-line kite. The best way involves having a friend help. Have your friend hold the kite while you walk off and take up a position with a reel in each hand. At a signal, you jerk on the line and your friend lets go of the kite. If the wind and other conditions are right, the kite should slip straight up into the blue. If it fails to rise despite considerable wind, try altering the tow points. And don't forget the possibility of adding a streamer tail if the kite proves unstable in the air.

An alternate launching method involves three people: one to hold the kite and the other two to hold a reel each while standing at some distance apart from each other. When the kite is in the sky, the reel holders should gradually walk toward each other.

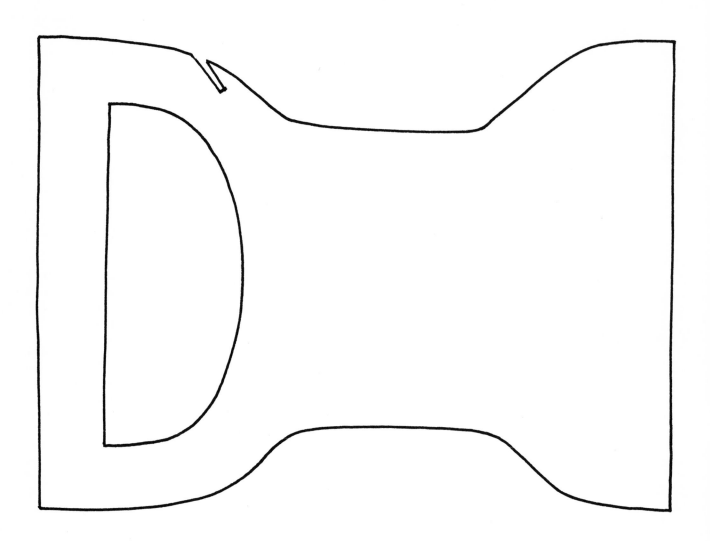

Fig. 3.9. Actual-size pattern for a plywood "slip reel."

Fig. 4.1. The Oriental Butterfly Kite.

4. The Oriental Butterfly Kite

THE ORIENTAL BUTTERFLY KITE is as unusual in its design as it is beautiful (see Fig. 4.1). Its shape is determined by two loops of cane held under tension by thin cord braces. It is meant rather for lazy, hazy flying than for fancy maneuvering, and yet it is sturdier than it looks. Special materials required for this kite include two lengths of rattan cane, 6′ long by ¼″ thick; colored tissue paper; and a selection of water-based inks in various colors. Be sure to select smooth, springy, straight-grained canes of a clear buff color.

Making the Frame

Rattan, unlike bamboo, will bend without steaming. Soak your two pieces overnight. Now take one of the soaked lengths of rattan and carefully bend it into a full circle. Overlap the ends and temporarily bind them together with twine. Then take the second cane and bend it into a shape as nearly identical with the first as possible. The hoops thus formed should be about 2′ in diameter (see Fig. 4.2).

Now place the rattan hoops on your work surface and overlap them as shown in Figs. 4.2 and 4.3 (the temporary lashings should be on the outer sides of the hoops). The "X" joints thus formed should be about 16″ apart. When you are sure that the frame is symmetrical, lash the "X"s with damp binding twine. Let dry, and dribble a little resin glue on the lashings (Fig. 4.4).

With the hoops thus joined and placed flat on your work surface, take a sufficient length of dampened twine and tie it to the frame of the left hoop just below the bottom "X"

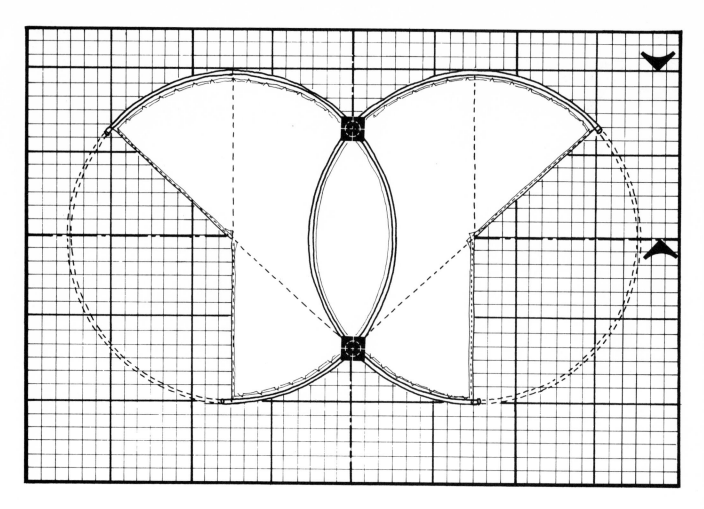

Fig. 4.2. Grid for measuring. Same scale as Fig. 2.4.

(see Fig. 4.5). Then stretch it across the exact center of the hoop and tie it firmly to the other side of the hoop. Repeat for the right hoop (see Fig. 4.3). Now tie on two more braces, this time in a vertical position; make sure that these also pass through the centers of the hoops. When the twine has dried, dribble resin glue over the knots.

Now, with these twine braces in place, you need to cut away parts of the frame to achieve the butterfly shape. The sections to be cut away are shown by double broken lines in Fig. 4.2. Cut away the cane to within an inch of the brace knots. The joined hoops will now be held in shape by the tension of the braces.

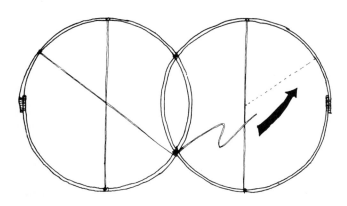

Fig. 4.3. Placing and bracing the hoops.

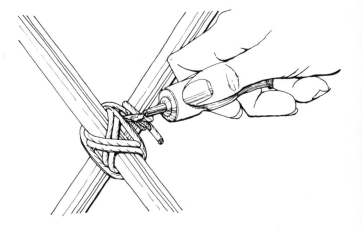

Fig. 4.4. Dribbling resin glue over a lashing.

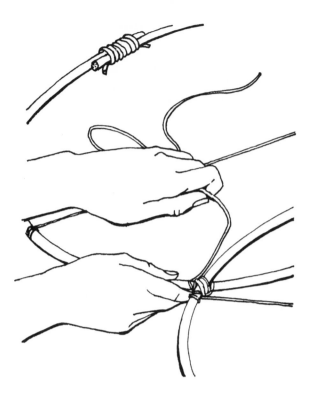

Fig. 4.5. Building the frame.

Making the Sail Cover

Use enough colored tissue paper to cover the frame and leave a 1″ margin when cutting around the frame (prepare the tissue paper as you did for the previous project and then place the frame over the tissue paper on your work surface; then cut). Where the paper is to be folded around a curved surface, knick "V"'s into the margin (see Fig. 4.2). Apply paste and carefully fold the paper over and smooth it down over the cane-and-twine frame (see Fig. 4.6).

In building this frame you may depart somewhat from the dimensions given, but always be careful to keep the two

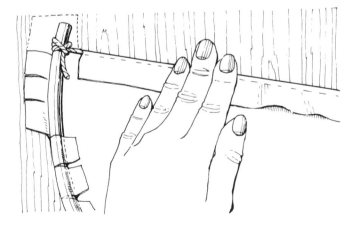

Fig. 4.6. Pasting on the sail cover.

sides symmetrical so the kite will fly properly. Remember too that weight is a critical factor: don't overbuild, and avoid huge, clumsy knots and extra-heavy borders.

Decorating the Sail Cover

Place the kite frame-side-down on your work surface. This kite, to be authentic, should be colored to resemble a butterfly. First draw in the outline of the pattern, using pencil, or, for a bolder effect, a felt-tip pen. Then fill in the colors by applying inks with brushes (Fig. 4.7). Create different color intensities by diluting the inks with water, holding

Fig. 4.7. Painting the sail cover.

different strengths in little dishes—or ink in the surfaces with full-strength inks first, and then apply water to "bleed." While the design should suggest a butterfly, do not strive for realism. The cleaner and bolder the lines, the better. Fig. 4.1 and the color illustration on the cover will give you an idea for one workable design. When you are satisfied with the appearance of the design, let the ink dry and apply a couple of coats of clear varnish or similar medium.

The Tail

The tail may be of any suitable lightweight, strong material. The traditional tail, illustrated here, is made of a 16′ length of strong cotton twine and about 50 bows of twisted paper, tied into the twine, three to the foot or so, with clove hitches. Tie one end securely to the lower of the "X"'s in the frame. It is a good idea to make an extra length of tail, to be added if the kite proves unstable in the air.

The Bridle, Line, and Reel

A simple two-leg bridle with a sliding-ring tow point works well with this kite. About 4′ of cord attached to the two "X"s will do the trick. Any strong, smooth, lightweight line will do for flying line, and a simple reel is all that is needed. Another idea for a reel is illustrated in Fig. 4.8. This one uses two flat pieces of wood and three dowels.

Flying the Oriental Butterfly Kite

Do not expect to accomplish dazzling feats of flying with this kite. It is meant for relatively low flying, but it presents a very striking appearance that will be sure to attract attention. If it fails to fly easily, experiment with different tail lengths and/or adjustments of the tow point.

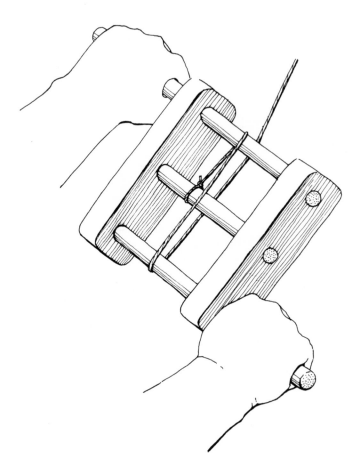

Fig. 4.8. A dowel-and-wood-block reel.

5. The Korean Warrior Kite

Fig. 5.1. The Korean Warrior Kite.

LIKE ITS NEIGHBORS China and Japan, Korea has a rich tradition of kite flying; kites are flown on ceremonial occasions, and kite fighting is a very popular sport. Korean kites conform more or less to a single pattern, having a four- or five-spar frame and a rectangular sail cover with a central hole and "sun disk" designs, and no tail. The Korean Warrior Kite you will make here has an added feature: you can take it apart, carry it easily to the field, and reassemble it on the spot. It is sturdily constructed of highly durable materials and is especially suited for strong winds, a very lively performer all in all.

In preparing to make this tough, easy-to-disassemble kite you should have a sewing machine, a pair of drawing compasses, and a very heavy needle with a large eye for thread-ing cotton tape (sailmaker's needle or bodkin). You will need 22' of cotton tape or cord and four cotton bootlaces. Use wooden dowels for the five spars. Obtain one $5/16''$ thick and 38'' long; two $5/16''$ thick and 45'' long; and two $1/4''$ thick and 27'' long. The sail cover is made of a 26'' × 38'' piece of lightweight cotton, nylon, or plastic fabric. You will also need a few (preferably brightly colored) pieces of the same type of fabric for the decorations and "ears"—what this kite uses as a stabilizer in place of a tail.

When you buy dowels, look for lengths that are slightly longer than the finished size—you can always cut them down. Avoid pieces with dark knots, split ends, or surface cracks.

Making the Frame Spars

Be sure your dowels have been cut to their proper lengths. Then rub them with a fine-grade sandpaper until they are smooth and free from splinters. Check the measurements once again (see Fig. 5.2), and be sure the dowels are quite smooth to the touch. Now, carefully label the spars as shown in Fig. 5.3. The 45″ dowels will become the diagonal spars; the 27″ dowels, the top and middle spars; and the 38″ dowel, the vertical spar. These are permanent labels for use in assembling the kite, so use indelible markers.

Now use a bootlace to lash the spars. Tie the two diagonals together first, and then add to these the vertical spar and middle spar (see Fig. 5.4). Then use the other three laces to lash the top spar to the top ends of the others (see Fig. 5.2). Use bows or slip knots. Do *not* use any glue! Remember: these lashings will never be permanent! They are made to be untied so that the kite can be taken apart, packed away, and later reassembled. Notice how the top spar holds the diagonals in place so that glue is not needed to fix the correct angles.

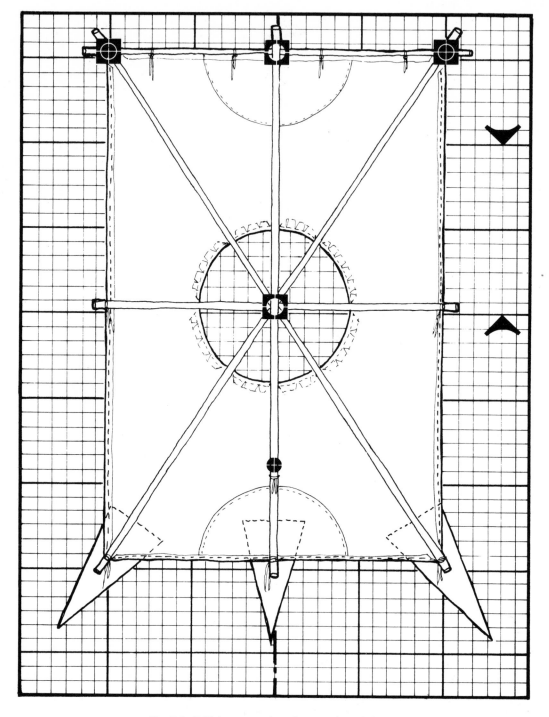

Fig. 5.2. Grid for measuring. Same scale as Fig. 2.4.

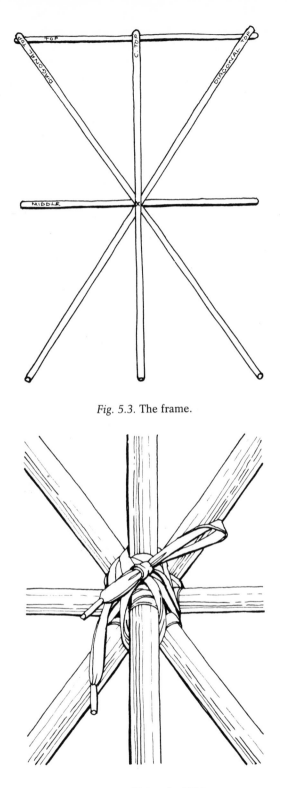

Fig. 5.3. The frame.

Fig. 5.4. Tying the "X."

Making the Sail Cover

The most important thing to remember when you are cutting your fabric is that you will be sewing a perimeter drawstring hem all around it. So make sure that this hem never gets blocked, which could accidentally occur, especially when you are sewing on the pieces of decorative fabric. Also be sure that this hem is large enough so you can easily pull the cotton-tape drawstring through it.

Cut out the fabric, fold over the material on all four sides for the hem, cut the corners, and tack around the hem with needle and tacking thread. Aim for a finished size of 24″ × 36″. This allows for a 1″ hem all around. Do not machine-sew at this time.

Now place the frame over the fabric, pencil-mark the position of the diagonal spars, and establish the exact center of the sail. This done, use the compasses to draw a circle on the fabric, 8″ in diameter. Cut this out. Nick "V" shapes about an inch deep around the circle and fold back the fabric. Tack down the circular hem thus created, so that the circular hole is about 10″ in diameter (see Fig. 5.2).

Now take a breather. Check all measurements. See that all is as it should be. When you are satisfied, use your sewing machine to sew around the perimeter drawstring hem and the circle hem. At this point you may block in the design on the sail cover, using felt-tip markers.

Take your extra fabric—scraps or whatever—and cut two circles, 10″ in diameter. These will create a really striking effect when seen from a distance if you use red fabric as we have done, but follow your own taste. Fold the circles around the top and bottom of the sail cover and tack them in place (Fig. 5.2), then machine-sew them (Fig. 5.5). Remember, do not sew over the drawstring hem! Now, with this caution in mind, cut out and sew on the three "ears" (Fig. 5.2).

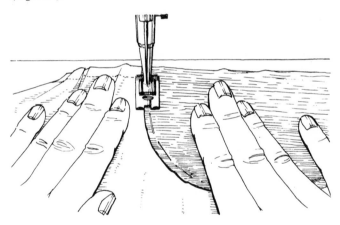

Fig. 5.5. Sewing on a circle.

This is a good time to sew a tape tie onto the fabric (exactly where the lower part of the middle spar will be) and, above it, a small brass or buttonhole eyelet (so the central bridle leg can pass through; see Figs. 5.1 and 5.2).

Now it is time to thread your sailmaker's (or equivalent large-eyed) needle with the cotton tape and insert the tape into the drawstring hem. Place the fabric on your work surface hem-side-up. Begin at the bottom, in the center. Pierce the fabric (not all the way through, of course, but just into the hem) and pull the needle through the hem until you have reached a corner. Pull the needle out and then, on the other side of where the diagonal spar is to be attached, reinsert it. Move the needle up to where the middle spar is

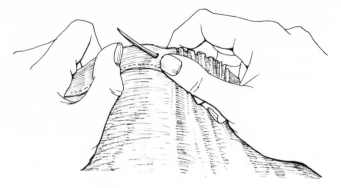

Fig. 5.6. Threading the hem.

to be attached, pull it out and in again in a similar manner, and so work your way around the perimeter (see Fig. 5.6). Leave about 12″ of tape outside each of these tie points as you go. Notice that, besides the eight tie points necessitated by the spar ends, there are four additional tie points along

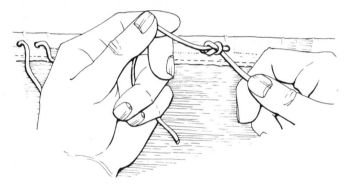

Fig. 5.7. Tying the tape.

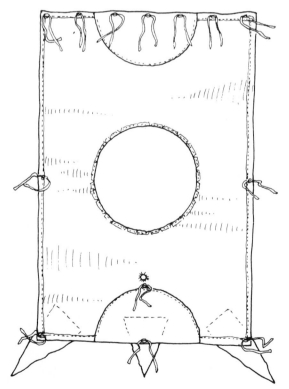

Fig. 5.8. The completed sail cover.

the top, where the top spar is to be attached. Except at the bottom center point (the beginning and ending point), you will have to cut the protruding tape in half at each tie point. You should be left with two 6″ lengths of tape at each of the twelve points. Tie each pair of tape lengths together (see Fig. 5.7). Your finished sail cover should have all the features shown in Fig. 5.8. When you are satisfied, fill in the design with bold blocks of color, using waterproof marking pens (see Fig. 5.9).

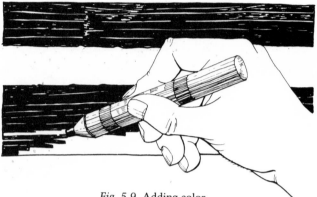

Fig. 5.9. Adding color.

The Bridle

When you have attached the sail cover to the frame (see below), you can rig up an effective three-point, three-leg bridle as follows. Take two lengths of cord, each 60″ long, and a tow ring. Tie one end of one of the pieces of cord to one of the two tie points at the upper left- and right-hand corners, and the other end to the other tie point. Do not attach it to the ring. Now take the other cord and, pulling it through the eyelet on the vertical spar, tie one end onto the spar. Take the other end and pull it through the tow ring. Wrap it around the ring a couple of times; then tie it onto the middle of the other cord. This will create a three-leg bridle that can be adjusted by sliding the tow ring up or down.

The Flying Line and Reel

This is a lively kite and can fly pretty high, so you should use plenty of fairly strong line. A good line to use is the twisted, multistranded plastic fishing line used by seashore anglers. It is usually three-ply and about 1/16″ thick, and is often colored bright orange. If you buy enough of it, it will probably come on a drum, which you can use for a reel. It never hurts to have extra line, so consider this. In any case, line of this nature is bulky, so you will need to hold it on a large reel.

Assembling and Flying the Korean Warrior Kite

If you have carefully followed our instructions in building the Korean Warrior, you should have no trouble assembling it in the field. Still, it is worthwhile having a couple of dry runs at home. On your launch site, if you are assembling this kite for the first time, it is easy enough to make a mistake when flies are buzzing, children are watching, and the wind is whistling in your ears! When putting together the frame, remember to join the diagonals first. Also, don't knot the bootlaces so you can't untie them later!

When the frame has been assembled, place the sail cover hem-side-up on a flat surface. Position the frame squarely over the sail, with all parts facing the right way. Knot the corner ties first. Then, working your way around the frame, knot the other ties (don't forget the one on the middle spar, near the center bridle tie point). As you tie on the sail, smooth it out, and, as necessary, adjust and reknot the ties to ensure that the sail is stretched evenly over the frame, with the cotton-tape drawstring evenly taut on all sides.

The kite having been satisfactorily assembled, tie on the bridle, attach the line, and you are ready to go. This kite can be launched without a helper, but if you have someone to help, you can make it easier by using the two-man launch method we described in Chapter 3. If the kite fails to take to the air at first try, give little jerks on the line and gradually work the kite higher. Don't forget your field kit. And bring plenty of spare line. There is nothing more frustrating than seeing your line come to an end just as your kite is really starting to climb!

6. The Chinese Yüan Kite

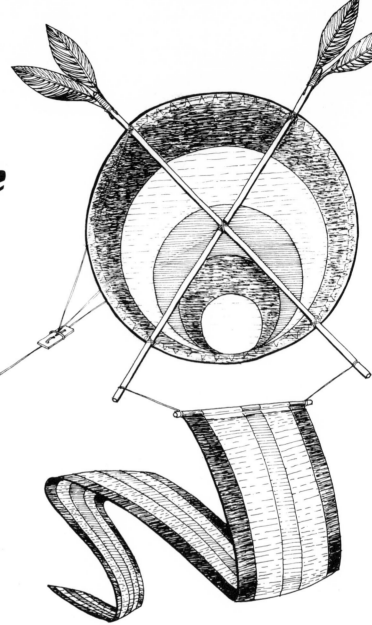

Fig. 6.1. The Chinese Yüan Kite.

FROM BAMBOO, rattan, and paper, the Chinese have over the course of centuries created some of the world's most unusually shaped and brightly colored kites. The Yüan Kite (*yüan* means "round"), with its round sail, feathered stabilizers, and flapping banner tail, is an impressive sight indeed. The Chinese traditionally make the sail cover of mulberry paper. This material is very expensive and hard to find, so we've substituted ordinary wall-lining paper. This is the paper that is sometimes used between the wall and the wallpaper itself. It is light, has considerable wet-strength, will shrink and stretch evenly, and has the particular advantage of being available everywhere. If you obtain a length in a white, cream, or neutral color, you can color it any way you choose. You'll need a piece measuring 30″ × 30″ for the sail cover and a long section—measuring roughly 10″ by 15′—for the banner tail. It is a good idea simply to purchase a whole roll in a standard 40″ or 46″ width. Tail length isn't critical, but it should be at least seven or eight times the diameter or length of the sail cover (which in this kite will be 24″).

Unlike our other kites, the Yüan has a frame combining both bamboo and rattan canes. You'll need two 36″ bamboo canes for the straight cross-spars, and a 12″ length of bamboo for the banner tail. The hoop is made of about 80″ of pencil-thick rattan (better to buy longer than shorter—you can always trim it down). You will also need feathers for the stabilizers, clear plastic adhesive tape, a tape measure, and the usual assortment of basic tools and materials we've used for the other kites.

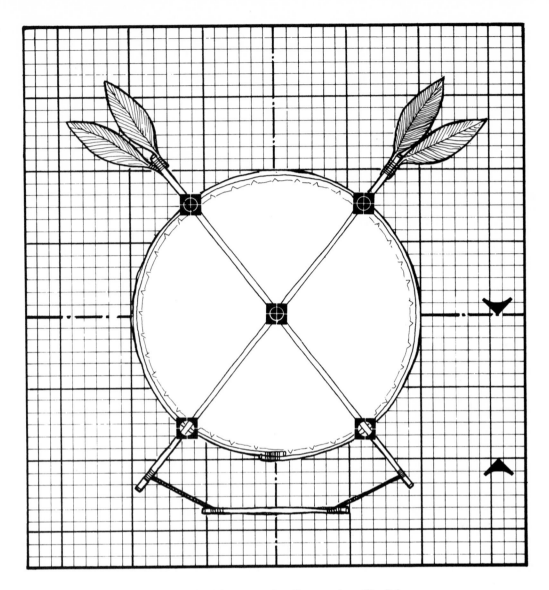

Fig. 6.2. Grid for measuring. Same scale as Fig. 2.4.

Making the Frame

Soak the rattan in water overnight. Cut and shape the ends as shown in Fig. 6.3. Work the cane into a circle, leaving an overlap of at least 2″ at the ends. Make sure the hoop you have formed is 24″ in diameter. Now, using sufficient dampened twine, bind the cut ends (as shown in Fig. 6.3). When the twine dries, it will pull the hoop ends firmly together.

Now, placing the hoop on your work surface, position the two bamboo cross-spars as indicated in Fig. 6.4. For balance and symmetry, be sure that the hoop joint is at the bottom. The spars should cross the hoop perimeter so they are about 15″ apart at the head and tail (see also Fig. 6.2). And be sure they cross each other at the exact center of the circle. When you are sure that all the parts of the frame are positioned properly, lash the center "X" and the four spar-hoop cross-points, using dampened twine. Allow to dry, and then dribble resin glue over all lashings and knots to add that extra measure of strength and durability.

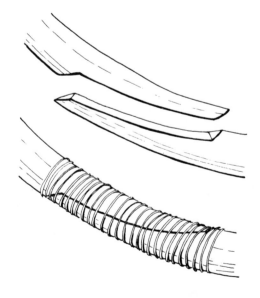
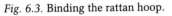

Fig. 6.3. Binding the rattan hoop.

Fig. 6.4. The frame.

Making the Sail Cover

Making the sail cover is a bit tricky, so work slowly and carefully. Place the wall-lining paper on your work surface and, using the assembled frame as a guide, measure a circle around the hoop. Mark the circle on the paper, adding a margin of 1″ all around. Cut this out. Make "V" notches in the margin and cut around the spar-hoop joints so that the margin area folds neatly over the hoop.

The next step is especially tricky, so be careful. You will need to have, within convenient reach, a bowl of water, a sponge, and a water-based paper paste or glue. Spread the cutout sail cover on a work surface that can take a drenching. Now saturate the paper with water. Using great care, sponge off the paper with a dabbing action. Wait a few minutes. The paper should expand evenly. Apply paste to the margin area and press down over the hoop edge. Try for a sail-cover margin that is neat, sharply defined, and wrinkle free. When you are satisfied with your efforts, lay the covered frame aside to dry, placing it flat, pasted side up. Make sure that it is not exposed to any sharp blasts of hot air while it is drying, which could cause it to warp.

The Banner; Decorations

Now cut out a strip of the wall-lining paper about 10″ wide and at least 15′ long. Apply paste to one end and wrap this end around the 12″ piece of bamboo, pasting it together and onto the cane (Fig. 6.5). Set this banner aside for the time being.

When the kite is thoroughly dry, and the sail-cover paper has shrunk tight as a drum over the frame, you are ready to

color the sail with inks and brushes. Any bright design will do, but you may wish to follow ours, which uses concentric circles (Fig. 6.1 and cover illustration). When you draw the outlines of these circles, be careful not to puncture the sail with the point of your compasses! Use the inks sparingly. If you work the ink with almost a "dry-brush" technique, you will achieve rich colors and a lively texture. Soaking the paper with inks should be avoided in any case, as this may cause warping.

After you have decorated the banner (with stripes or a design of your own choosing) and the ink has dried, reinforce the sides and bottom with continuous strips of clear, sticky tape (see Fig. 6.5).

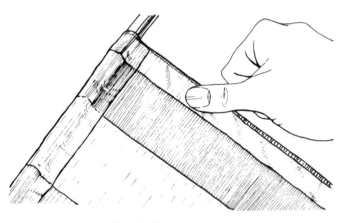

Fig. 6.5. The banner tail.

Now you can heave a sigh of relief. Your kite is almost complete! At this stage, you would do well to give the entire kite, banner and all, a couple of coats of plastic boat varnish. We have found that this treatment strengthens the kite structure, lends a parchmentlike appearance to the sail, and protects the kite from rain and puddles.

When the varnish has dried, attach feathers (or equivalent "ears") to the top of the spars, binding them as shown in Fig. 6.6. These ornaments will act as stabilizers. Finally, using two pieces of cord, attach the banner tail to the bottom of the spars as shown in Figs. 6.1 and 6.2. Make sure to tie it so it is balanced, hanging midway between the spars.

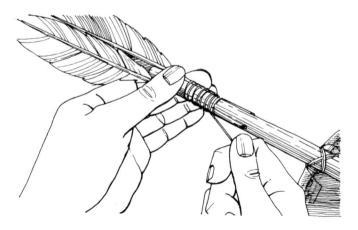

Fig. 6.6. Binding the feathers.

The Bridle

This kite is best flown with a three-leg bridle and metal-plate tow point. The two outer legs are made of a continuous length of cord, each end of which is tied on at a spar-frame junction point (Figs. 6.1 and 6.2) and the middle of which is passed through and around the tow plate (Fig. 6.7). The center leg of the bridle, attached to the "X" (be careful piercing the sail), is actually an extension of the flying line. Pass it through the plate as shown in Fig. 6.7. A three-ply plastic line of medium weight works well with this kite. The center bridle leg can be shortened simply by sliding up the tow plate. The outer legs can be shortened by pulling out and knotting off the loop that this part of the bridle makes as it runs over the tow plate (Fig. 6.7).

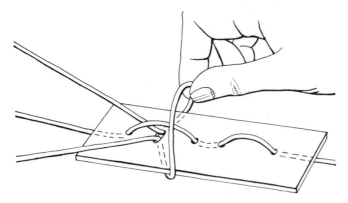

Fig. 6.7. The bridle tow plate.

The Reel

Fig. 6.8 provides working drawings for a very effective reel for use with this kite. This reel may seem excessively large. But when you realize that it lets out or hauls in at least 24″ of line with each revolution, you will understand its great advantage over smaller reels. And it handles very easily.

You will need two 12″-diameter disks of ½″-thick plywood; three 1″-diameter, 6″-long dowels; two 1″-diameter, 9″- or 10″-long dowels; a cardboard-tube sleeve about 5″ long, to fit over one of the latter dowels; two bicycle handles (handgrips) to fit over the ends of these longer dowels; four wooden washers; and two split pins.

Drill the holes and glue in the shorter dowels as shown in Fig. 6.8. Attach the bicycle handles to the two longer dowels. Insert these in place, using the wooden washers and, on the outside dowel, the cardboard-tube sleeve. Drill holes for the split pins through the dowels and insert the pins. These handle-dowels should end up about 12″ long each. They should turn freely in their holes, so be sure you have made the holes large enough. Note that one of these handle-dowels goes in the center, while the other is placed so that, seen from the side, its end makes a square with the ends of the short dowels (Fig. 6.8).

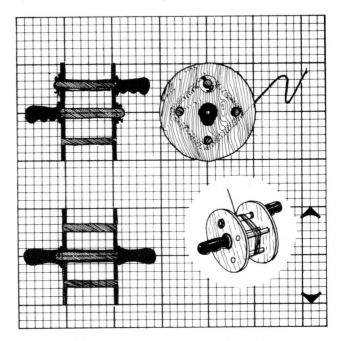

Fig. 6.8. Working drawings for a reel. Grid is same scale as Fig. 2.4.

When you have assembled the reel and the glue has dried (do not glue the handle-dowels!), remove the handle-dowels and use sandpaper to give the whole reel a smooth finish. Then apply a couple of coats of varnish and let dry. (The cardboard-tube sleeve on the outer handle-dowel prevents binding and friction.)

Flying the Chinese Yüan Kite

The Yüan is best flown in a light-to-moderate breeze. If it bucks or staggers in flight, adjust the bridle. If this fails to help, try adding stabilizer feathers or even tassel side drags.

7. The Guatemalan Sun Kite

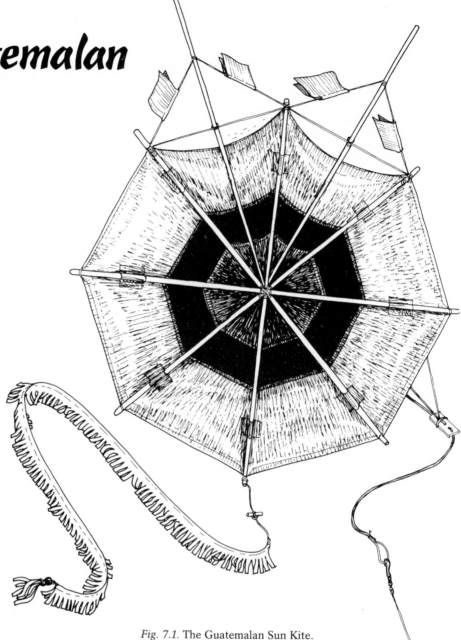

Fig. 7.1. The Guatemalan Sun Kite.

IN BERMUDA, the Caribbean, and Central America, large hexagonal and octagonal kites are an important part of folk festivals. They are flown, among other occasions, to welcome the "season of the sun"—hence the name "sun" kite. This version of the Guatemalan Sun Kite has been somewhat modernized: we have used plastic film for the sail cover. The spars, however, are of the traditional bamboo, and the design is a traditional one.

Despite its apparent complexity, you will not find this kite difficult to make unless you have trouble splitting bamboo—about the trickiest part of making this high flier. Besides performing well, the Guatemalan Sun Kite "sings": it has four easy-to-make "buzzers" that vibrate in the wind and create a music of their own!

The structure is as follows. The sail cover is supported by four main spars; two shorter "outrigger" spars provide the means for attaching the buzzers; and there are a tail and a three-leg bridle. Besides many of the usual tools and materials, you will need two 1″-thick, 40″-long bamboo canes and one slightly thinner, 30″-long bamboo cane; a 48″ × 48″ sheet of plastic film; a couple of smaller pieces of the same material in different colors, for decorations; about 12′ of strong cotton or linen twine for the frame; 20′ or 25′ of suitable cord for the tail; a roll of 2″-wide plastic tape of the strong kind used for wrapping parcels; and a roll of tape that is sticky on both sides.

When purchasing the bamboo, avoid canes that are green or dark brown; also, they should not sound shattered when you tap them on the ground.

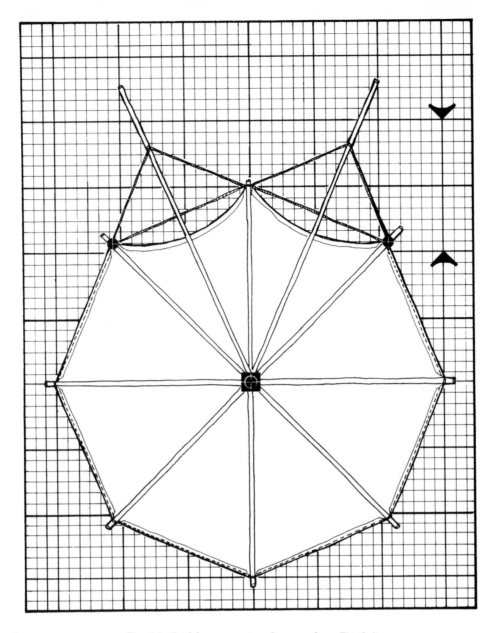

Fig. 7.2. Grid for measuring. Same scale as Fig. 2.4.

Making the Frame

Split the bamboo canes as you did those for the European Diamond Kite (Chapter 2, above). Use a sharp, heavy knife and follow the grain of the bamboo, using a twisting motion. Passing the nodes will be a bit more difficult than the rest. Go slowly, with a seesawing motion (Fig. 7.3). The nodes are also the place to adjust the direction of the cut if you feel it going off. If the blade gets stuck, and nothing else works, you might try tapping it with a mallet. Once the canes have been split, go over them and trim off all splinters and sharp edges, without cutting away all the curves. Finally, smooth the canes with a fine grade of sandpaper. Check to see if any of the resulting half-canes are heavier at one end; if so, when constructing the frame, place the heavier ends towards what will be the bottom of the kite.

Now you are ready to lash the spars together. With dampened twine, lash a central "X"; now to this lash another "X" with the half-canes facing the other way and at a 45° angle to the first "X" (Fig. 7.4). Fix the spars so they are evenly spaced. Now tie on the frame line. Dampen the twine and tie it from spar end to spar end, making adjustments as you go and keeping the line taut. Strive for a symmetrical, balanced design, as shown in Fig. 7.5, with the spar ends about 14" apart at the tie points.

You are now ready to attach the outrigger spars. Carve little necks or hollows into all lash points and then lash them onto the central "X" (Fig. 7.4) and tie them to the frame line. Now add braces that run from near the ends of the outriggers to the ends of the top three main spars. Also attach two loose secondary lines between these main spars (see Fig. 7.5).

When you are sure that everything is in order, dribble a little resin glue on all knots and lashings.

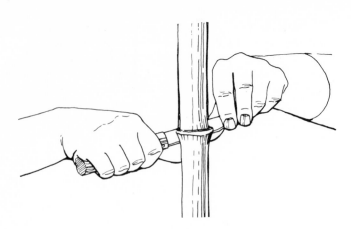

Fig. 7.3. Splitting the cane.

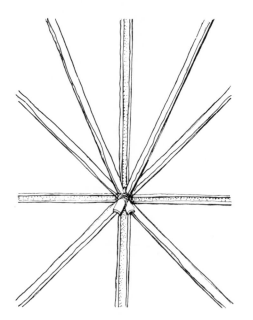

Fig. 7.4. The central "X."

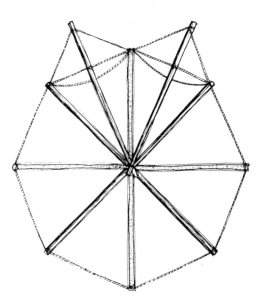

Fig. 7.5. The frame.

Making the Sail Cover

Spread out the large sheet of plastic film and position the kite frame squarely over it. Allowing for a 1″-margin flap around the frame, mark and cut out the sail cover. Cut around the spars and then paste down the flaps with the 2″-wide tape. The two uppermost flaps should go over the two loose secondary frame lines, forming "vent-pocket" panels. These should be secure yet slack-edged (see Fig. 7.6). Use tape also in the middle of the main spars to strengthen their attachment to the sail cover (Fig. 7.1).

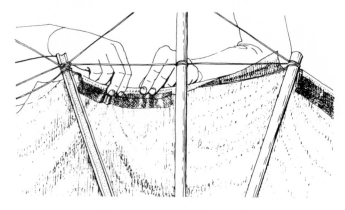

Fig. 7.6. A vent-pocket panel.

Decorating Your Guatemalan Sun Kite

This kite is decorated by applying to the sail cover colored patches of the plastic film. As you can see (Fig. 7.1), we have superimposed two octagonal patches concentrically in the exact center of the sail cover. These are secured by placing the double-sided sticky tape between layers. You can vary the decorations if you wish, but it is important to remember that the decorations must be symmetrical to keep the sail cover balanced. Each added layer of material contributes weight to the kite, and this weight must be distributed evenly on both sides.

Now attach the "buzzers." These are simply four pieces of the plastic cut from scrap (all cut to exactly the same size—remember the importance of balance!), each folded over an outrigger brace line and pasted together, just below the fold, with a strip of double-sided sticky tape (see Fig. 7.7).

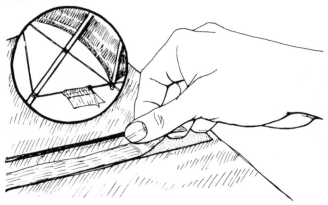

Fig. 7.7. Attaching a buzzer.

Making the Tail

For the tail you will need 20' to 25' of suitable cord. Now take all your scraps of plastic and cut them into 6"-wide strips. Fold these over the cord to make a continuous strip. Secure this over the cord with the double-sided sticky tape, as you did the buzzers. With scissors, cut fringes into this strip (Fig. 7.8). As you will want to adjust the length of the tail or even remove the whole thing for repairs, it is a good idea to construct the tail of separate lengths joined together and to the kite by toggles and loops. (see Fig. 7.1).

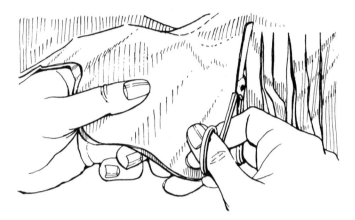

Fig. 7.8. Cutting fringes in the tail.

The Bridle, Flying Line, and Reel

This kite uses a three-leg bridle with a metal-plate tow point, the type of bridle we used with the Chinese Yüan Kite (see last chapter). You will need bridle cords about 8' long. With this kite we suggest attaching the center leg to the flying line with a loop and a clip-and-swivel (Fig. 7.9). Attach the bridle legs at the points marked in Fig. 7.2. As always, be careful when piercing the sail cover.

You may want to experiment with different types and weights of flying line. In any case, use plenty—this kite is potentially a high flier. A reel of the type described in the last chapter works very well with this kite.

Fig. 7.9. Loop and clip-and-swivel bridle-to-flying-line attachment.

Flying the Guatemalan Sun Kite

Give this kite plenty of room and plenty of flying line, and it will reach considerable heights, buzzing and whistling all the way. Make the usual tail and bridle adjustments as necessary. You will know when the kite has reached its limit because the line will sag and drag the kite back down. Be ready for any problems, so bring those extra lengths of tail and your complete "Kite Kit."

8. The Traditional Chinese Dragonfly Kite

Fig. 8.1. The Traditional Chinese Dragonfly Kite.

MANY TRADITIONAL Chinese kites are shaped like butterflies, birds, or dragonflies. They have delicate, multisectioned cane frames, and their light tissue-paper sails are decorated with brightly colored designs painted with beautiful brushwork. The Dragonfly Kite you will make from the instructions in this chapter closely follows the tradition. Its frame is much more intricately constructed than those of the other kites in this book, even the Oriental Butterfly. It is a beautiful kite that can be hung on the wall as a decoration. Yet it is also very much a working kite that can be flown, although it is not a high flier. Its essential features are form, color, and adherence to traditional style. If you are interested in the ethnic and artistic—as distinguished from the aerodynamic—aspects of kites, then you will enjoy working on this project.

Structured somewhat like a ship, the frame of the Dragonfly has a hull, ribs, and a keel, all made of rattan. It is

difficult to say in advance how much rattan you will need—you may have to add extra ribs and there will probably be a fair amount of wastage—but, roughly speaking, you should have on hand about 20′ or 25′ altogether. Of this quantity, the longest single piece will measure 76″; you will also need two pieces about 45″, and one about 36″ long. The diameter of the cane should be about ⅛″ to ¼″. Your work surface for this project should be one on which you can pin down portions of the frame (for which you will need dressmaker's pins).

The sail cover is made of several pieces of strong tissue paper pasted together over the various parts of the frame. You will need about 8 or 9 square feet of the kind of tissue paper used by paper-airplane makers. Again, it is impossible to figure the exact amount because of a certain inevitable quantity of waste. You will also need a water-based paste suited to this tissue paper. If you have brushes and inks, fine cotton thread, a place for soaking the rattan in hot water, and the usual other tools and materials, you will have what you need to get started building the Chinese Dragonfly Kite.

Building the Frame

You will notice that the cross sections in Fig. 8.2 show three alternate ways of building the wing-spars-and-ribs. You may experiment with the top two, but we feel that the bottom design is the best all-around, and this is the design we follow in these instructions.

Each wing-spar-and-rib consists of two pieces of cane lashed with fine cotton thread. To begin, cut two pieces of cane, one about 40" long, the other about 18" long. Mark the longer piece with a pencil, exactly at its midpoint. Soak the canes in hot water for a few minutes (a bathtub may be the most convenient place!). When the cane is pliable—when it bends without cracking—remove the long piece and bend it carefully into the spar-and-rib shown in Fig. 8.3. The center portion should form a loop, and the "wings" should form a slight dihedral angle. With fine cotton thread, lash the loop at the bottom cross-point, which should be the exact center of the cane. Now take the shorter piece of rattan, bend it to form a bridge, and lash it in four places as shown in Fig. 8.2.

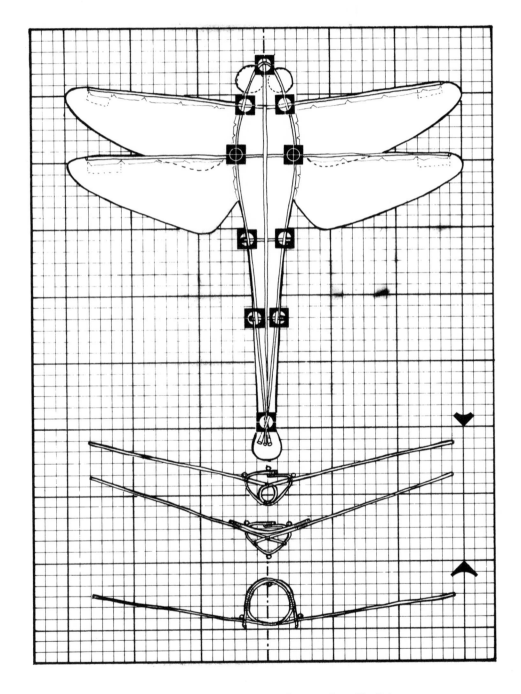

Fig. 8.2. Grid for measuring. Same scale as Fig. 2.4.

Fig. 8.3. Forming the wing-spar-and-rib.

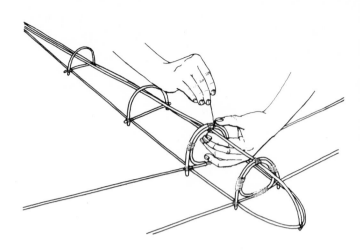

Fig. 8.5. The hull.

Lash it so that the bridge surrounds and braces the loop. The bridge also should fix the dihedral angle. This angle is correct if, when the bottom of the spar-and-loop is placed on a flat surface, the spar tips rise to about 3″ above the surface. Bend the spar so the ends point slightly forward as well (forward, that is, when seen from *above*); see Fig. 8.2. This is all easier to do than to describe. When you are satisfied that the shape and angles are right, pin this spar-and-rib into position on your work surface (Fig. 8.4) and let it dry.

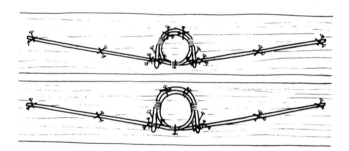

Fig. 8.4. Pinning down the spars to dry.

Now make another wing-spar-and-rib. This one should have a slightly larger loop (so you will need a slightly longer piece of rattan) and its spar ends, while fixed at the same dihedral angle, should not point forward when seen from above (Fig. 8.2). Now, when you are sure it has been bent and lashed correctly, pin this down to dry as well.

Now you can make the "hull" of your kite. Soak a piece of cane about 76″ long. Bend it loosely in half so that the ends meet. Lash these ends together with the cotton twine. Now line up the wing spars. Place the wing spar with the smaller loop toward the front and the other wing spar toward the back. These will be perpendicular to the hull spars. Next, take the long, bent piece of rattan and, gently pulling out its sides, slide it over the wing-spar loops, until it comes to rest on the spars, positioning the spars as shown in the diagrams (Figs. 8.2 and 8.5). The hull frame should have

just enough tension to grip the wing-spar loops. Lash the wings to the hull. At this point, when you place the structure on your work surface with the loops on top, it should lie flat and the wings should rise slightly, their tips ending about 3″ above the work surface.

Now you will have to add at least two (three or four if you find it necessary) rib-bracers; for each of these you will need one short, straight piece of rattan and a longer, curved piece (see Fig. 8.5). Take a good look at the structure, and if you think it needs braces at any point, now is the time to lash them on. Finally, take a long piece of cane and bend it so it forms a central spine or "keel." Lash this to the front of the hull, to the center of each rib, and to the tail (Fig. 8.5). You can now add two rattan "eye" loops (Fig. 8.6).

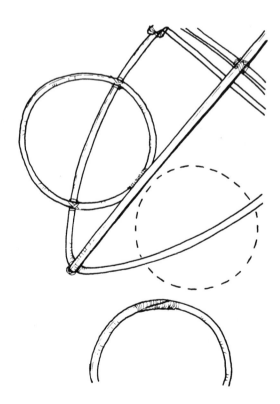

Fig. 8.6. The eye loops.

Step back at this point and check the whole frame for symmetry and balance. Make sure everything is as it should be. The frame should look rather like an upside-down rowboat with two pairs of oars sticking out. When you are sure that all is correct, dribble a little resin glue over all lashings, and set aside to dry.

Covering the Frame

Covering the frame is a trickier operation with this kite than with the others. Still, it should present no major difficulties if you work slowly, step by step. To cover the hull, you will need a sufficient number of 4″-wide strips of tissue paper. Apply the paste with a brush where needed. Wrap the strips around the hull like bandages, overlapping one another. Each strip should overlap itself slightly so its ends can be pasted together. Be sure to account for all of this when cutting out the strips (see Fig. 8.7).

Try to work the strips over all joints and protrusions to create a smooth, skinlike appearance. Use small pieces around the eyes. When you come to the dragonfly's head, cut out several disks of tissue paper and paste them in layers over the nose to reinforce it. Now set the frame aside to dry slowly before you create the wings.

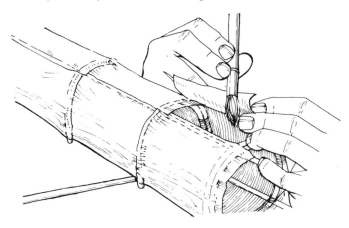

Fig. 8.7. Covering the hull.

Take special care over this next stage of operation. Do one wing at a time. Place the frame over a large sheet of the tissue paper. Draw the wing shape on the paper, including the outline of the trailing edge, which is not part of the frame (see Fig. 8.2 for the shape). Add a margin around the wing perimeter. Cut out this shape.

The margin flap along the leading edge of the wing (the part defined by the wing spar) should be pasted down first. "V"-cut into sections to make this easier (see Fig. 8.8). Do as smooth and even a job as you can. Do not proceed immediately to pasting down the trailing edge—as yet there is nothing to paste it to. Take a sufficient length of fine cotton thread, knot and glue it to the spar end, and lay it along the perimeter of the wing's trailing edge, but inside the margin flap. (Actually, this reinforcement first extends the wing's leading edge before looping around to become the trailing edge; see Fig. 8.8). Now "V"-cut, apply paste to, and fold over the margin flap (Fig. 8.8). The thread-

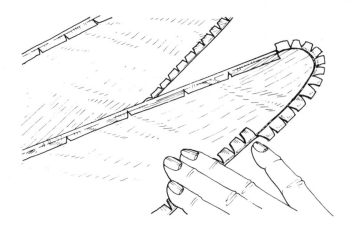

Fig. 8.8. Covering the wings.

reinforced edge of the wing should be well shaped and even. Make sure also that a margin of the tissue paper is neatly and smoothly pasted onto the hull where the hull is joined by the base of the wing. All this will take time. Work slowly and carefully, and you will be proud of the results. When you have finished the first wing, proceed in turn to the three others. Let the completed tissue-paper-covered frame dry thoroughly.

Now stand back and examine your work. The four wings should have rattan leading edges and cotton-thread-reinforced trailing edges. The tissue-paper cover should flow smoothly over the ribs, eyes, tail, and wing-hull joints. The nose should be well reinforced. And all the elements should be in the right proportions, so the whole resembles a dragonfly. Test a final time for balance. The kite should not droop to one side when pivoted between your fingertips. If it shows an imbalance, add some tissue-paper-strip reinforcements under the wings on the lighter side.

Decorating Your Kite

You are now ready to think about the decoration. Clean off your work surface. Gather your waterproof inks and long-haired brushes. You may also want to use small dishes for diluting the inks with water.

Take some time to plan your color scheme. If you wish to develop your own dragonfly design, study color photographs and drawings of dragonflies in reference books. You may simply want to follow the color scheme we show here. In either case, remember that, as this kite is not shaped *exactly* like a dragonfly, neither should the color scheme be realistic to the last detail. Just pick out what you consider to be the most important characteristics, and capture the essential forms and colors. You can dilute inks with water to create lighter shades, if you wish. These may be used along with the full-strength inks for maximum variety of shading, the method we adopted for our coloring of the design.

Don't saturate the tissue when you are applying inks. Paint a single area or motif at a time, let this dry, and then go on to the next area. As the ink dries, it will tighten up the tissue paper and give it a slightly shiny finish. Normally kites of this kind are considered complete at this point, but you may want to experiment with a varnish finish or the like.

The Bridle, Flying Line, and Reel

This kite uses a very simple, two-leg bridle. Just tie a 3′–4′ length of cord to the bridle points (the two places where the rear wing spar crosses the hull frame—see Fig. 8.2), and use a metal-ring tow point (see Fig. 8.9). A medium-weight fishing line and a plywood slip reel, such as has been shown for the European Diamond Kite (Chapter 2), are suitable for this kite.

Flying the Traditional Chinese Dragonfly Kite

This kite isn't a high flier, but it certainly is an eye-catching sight in the air. Although it looks fragile, the Chinese Dragonfly is quite capable of surviving any number of crash landings in grassy meadows. Do avoid areas with thorny or sharp-edged plants, however, as you would when flying any kite. If the Dragonfly is nose-heavy, staggers, jerks to one side, or otherwise behaves badly in the air, and you can't solve the problem by adjusting the bridle, you can try adding a long streamer tail.

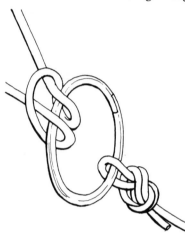

Fig. 8.9. The tow ring.

9. The New England Ghost Kite

Fig. 9.1. The New England Ghost Kite.

ON MOONLESS NIGHTS in rural New England, in other parts of America, and in parts of Europe, strange flashing objects have often been sighted in the sky. If the truth were told, many of these ghostly "UFOs" would probably turn out to have been Ghost Kites of the kind you will learn to make in this chapter. This dazzling kite is a favorite for nighttime flying, when a flashlight beam reflected from its shiny plastic surface can create a truly eerie effect. It can, however, be flown enjoyably at any time. With its dual flying lines, it is an excellent "swooper."

A helper—even better, two—makes both constructing and flying this kite a whole lot easier. It is not really difficult to put together and can be managed by one person working carefully, but that extra pair of hands does make a difference.

The New England Ghost Kite is as modern and Western as the Butterfly and Dragonfly kites are traditional and Eastern. The Ghost Kite (at least our version of it) has a frame of fiberglass rods and a sail cover of plastic film, with extra pieces of the plastic used for ornaments. The decoration is not painted on but inheres in the materials used in construction. For an even more showy effect you can use mirror plastic and colored tapes instead of the clear materials we have shown here. The New England Ghost Kite consists of several sections that you can take apart. This way it can be easily transported to the field and reassembled there.

Not many tools and materials are needed to make this kite. A few things are somewhat out of the ordinary. You will need fiberglass rods in seven lengths: one 48″, one 42″,

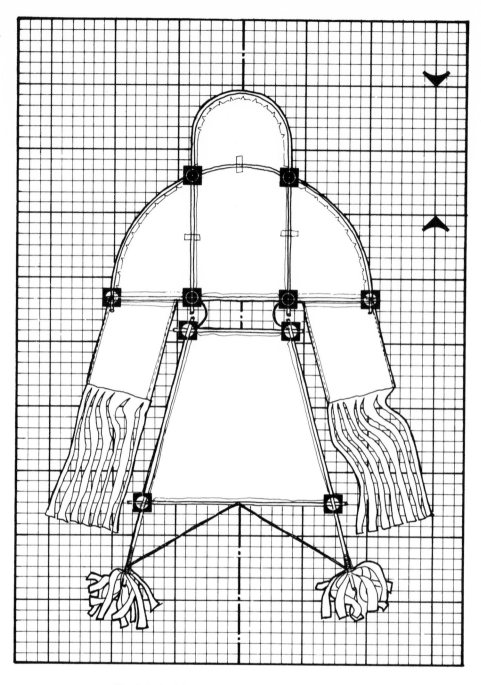

Fig. 9.2. Grid for measuring. Same scale as Fig. 2.4.

three 26″, one 20″, and one 12″. You will need a 48″ × 48″ sheet of plastic film, and enough strong clear adhesive tape for attaching the cut pieces of plastic to the fiberglass frame. A fine-tooth saw will be necessary to cut the fiberglass to size, and a fine grade of sandpaper to smooth it out.

Making the Frame

Be careful when sawing the fiberglass (Fig. 9.3). It is best to do all sawing and sandpapering at one sitting. Then clear away all bits and pieces and wipe down your work surface with a damp cloth. That way you will avoid getting dust in your eyes and splinters under your fingernails.

When you have cut the rods to size and sandpapered away all splinters and rough edges, you can begin to construct the main frame. Be careful bending the fiberglass rods. Reproduce the correct shapes, in the correct dimensions, as shown in Fig. 9.2. First bend the 42″ rod into a semicircle with a diameter of 24″. Lash to this one of the 26″ rods as shown in Fig. 9.2. Then bend the 48″ rod in half so it has two straight sides ending in a semicircle. Again, see Fig. 9.2. The straight sides should be 10″ apart. Temporarily tie cords across these sides, as shown in Fig. 9.4. Now lash the two part-frames together at the four points shown in Fig. 9.2. Be careful to lash them at exactly the right places. The four "X"s are also the four bridle points, so lash them neatly and securely. Remove the temporary cords. When

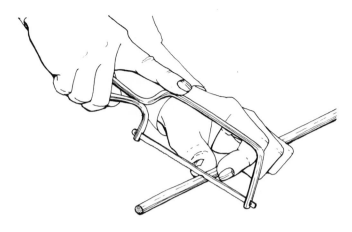

Fig. 9.3. Cutting a fiberglass rod.

you are satisfied that the part-frames have been lashed tightly and in the right places and that the frame is symmetrical, dribble some resin glue on the lashings.

Now you can make the "skirt" frame. For this, use the four remaining fiberglass rods. Lash them as shown in Fig. 9.2 and add the two cord bracers stretching from the center to just above the "feet."

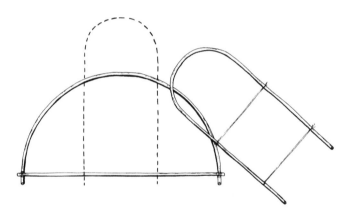

Fig. 9.4. The two parts of the head-and-shoulders frame.

Covering the Frame

The sail cover of this kite is in two main parts, one part covering the "head-and-shoulders" frame, the other the "skirt" frame. Lay out the sheet of plastic and, with little pieces of sticky tape, secure it in place on the work surface. Place the frames (separately) over the plastic film, and cut out the shapes, leaving margins all around. "V"-cut around the curves (see Fig. 9.5). Before you do the final pasting, use little tabs of tape to "tack" the sail cover in place. Smooth out rough edges and make sure the film is taut and even. Then smooth large strips of the tape in place to fasten the cover onto the frame permanently.

A word of caution. Both the tape and the plastic film generate large quantities of static electricity. This can cause the tape to slip out of your fingers and stick to the film in the wrong place before you have properly positioned the mate-

rials. Once this happens you will probably not be able to remove the tape and may ruin the whole project. Here especially it helps to have an assistant. One of you holds the film in place while the other carefully positions the tape.

Cover the "skirt" frame in a similar manner. When the kite is ready for test-flying, attach the skirt with cords to the

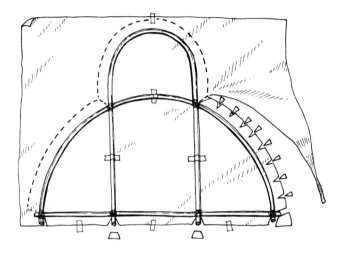

Fig. 9.5. Cutting out the sail cover.

head-and-shoulders. Notice that there are also two fringed "arm" flaps. These can be made of 6″-wide pieces of the plastic film, each about 2′ long. Reinforce the sides with cord and use tape along the top and bottom (above the fringes) as well as the sides. The fringes can simply be cut with scissors (see Fig. 9.6). It is a good idea, also, to trim the tops—before taping, of course—to cause the arms to swing outward, clear of the skirt (see Fig. 9.2).

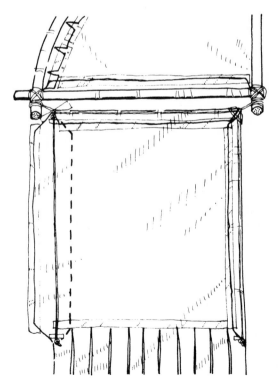

Fig. 9.6. Forming an arm.

The "feet" can be made of bunches of plastic scraps tied onto the legs of the skirt. Darker pieces of plastic may be pasted on the head for eyes. For easier detaching of cord-linked sections, you can use toggles-and-loops, as shown in Fig. 9.7.

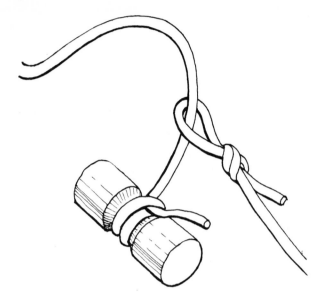

Fig. 9.7. A toggle-and-loop joint.

The Bridles, Flying Lines, and Reels

This kite is best flown with twin two-leg bridles, flying lines, and reels. For bridles, just attach two 5′ lengths of cord to the "neck" and "waist" bridle points (see Figs. 9.1 and 9.2). Use single-ring tow points and suitable flying lines. The flat plywood slip reels used for the European Diamond and Japanese Red Devil Swooper kites (Chapters 2 and 3) are excellent.

Flying the New England Ghost Kite

The three-man launch method (described at the end of Chapter 3) works best with this kite (see Fig. 9.8). For night flying you can have great fun by wearing a flashlight attached to a helmet (Fig. 9.9). This leaves both hands free to work the kite reels, while by looking up at the kite you can illuminate it with the beam of the flashlight.

Fig. 9.8. The three-man launch.

Fig. 9.9. Flying the New England Ghost Kite at night.

10. The High-Tech Box Kite

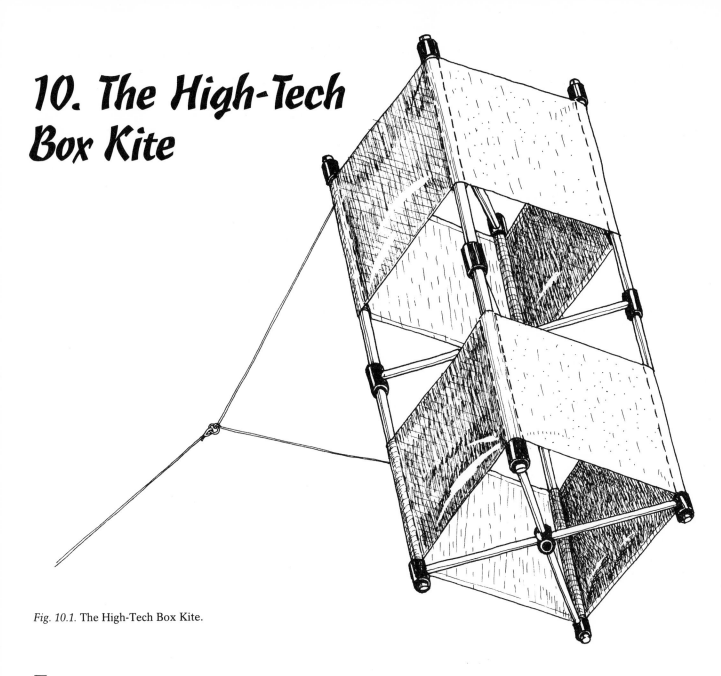

Fig. 10.1. The High-Tech Box Kite.

THE BOX KITE is the aristocrat of high-flying kites. In our high-tech version, we have combined the classic Hargrave design with the most modern materials—aluminum and plastic tubing, and synthetic fabric—to make a lightweight, sturdy, easily stored and reassembled kite that will withstand rough winds, climb rapidly, and reach impressive heights.

The structure of the High-Tech Box Kite is really very simple. The two "cells" are formed by two pieces of fabric wrapped around the four main spars. Three sets of cross-braces hold the shape of the kite and keep the fabric taut. Each set is made of two kinds of braces: one long, fixed brace that passes diagonally across the frame; and two half-braces, at right angles to the long brace, that are removable so that the frame can be collapsed for easy carrying. The stretch of the fabric enables the half-braces to be removed and replaced with all other elements in position.

To make this kite you will need access to a fine-tooth metalwork saw, a hand drill with a ⅜″ bit, and a sewing machine. The other tools are smaller: a file; emery paper; a good, sharp pair of scissors; and some other implements usually needed for kite making. The materials are relatively few and simple. You will need thirteen lengths of ⅜″-diameter aluminum tubing: four pieces 42″ long, three 18″ long, and six 9″ long. Make sure the tubing is free from bends, kinks, and dents. For the spar-brace joints, you will need 24″ of polyethylene tubing with an inside diameter of ⅜″ and an outside diameter of ⅝″–1″. For cutting this, you will need to use some scrap dowel that can be slipped inside of it. And you will need eight 13″ × 14″ pieces of a somewhat elastic, lightweight synthetic fabric, in two colors, of the kind used for tents and windsurfer sails. If you want sail covers in one color only, then you can start with two pieces measuring 13″ × 53″.

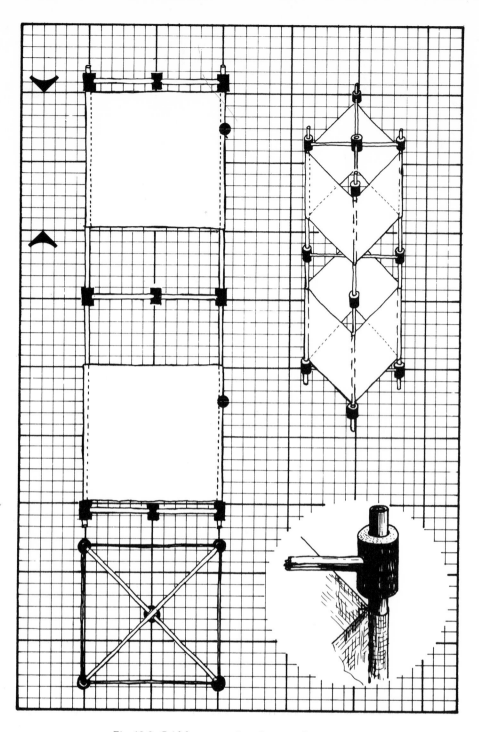

Fig. 10.2. Grid for measuring. Same scale as Fig. 2.4.

Making the Components

Measurements are critical for this kite, so take the time to measure and cut carefully. Prepare the aluminum tubing first. Cut the 42″ spars to size, and then file and rub down the ends so that they are smooth and free from burrs. In a similar manner, cut the brace and half-brace tubes. If you cut these a little longer than their final size, you can trim them down gradually to ensure a perfect fit.

Clean off your work surface, making sure that there are no aluminum splinters or filings left lying around. Now take the polyethylene tubing and mark it to be cut into 1½″ lengths. This will give you 15, plus one spare. Three of these will be the center joints. For these you need to drill four side holes. Do this as follows. Insert the scrap dowel in the tube. Brace the tube in a wood vise. With your hand drill and ⅜″ bit, drill two holes, all the way through the tube and dowel, at right angles to each other. Then drill the single holes in the remaining 12 joints (Fig. 10.3), trim off the burrs and ragged edges with a sharp knife and the emery paper, and cut out the joints. With the aluminum tubes, test the joints for fit (Fig. 10.4).

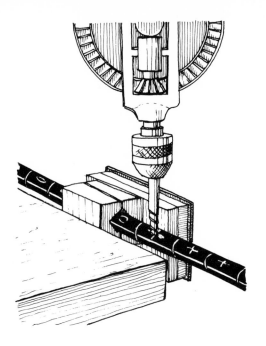

Fig. 10.3. Drilling the holes in the joints.

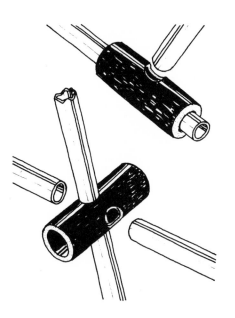

Fig. 10.4. Testing for fit.

Now lay aside the aluminum tubes and polyethylene joints. Clean up your work surface and set aside the metal-working tools. Set your sewing machine for a zigzag stitch. Take the eight 13″ × 14″ pieces of fabric, and tack and sew two ½″ hems on opposite sides of each piece (the resulting piece should measure 12″ × 14″). Now, alternating colors, tack and sew the pieces together in two groups of four each. Where the pieces are sewn together, leave ½″ of seam on each piece at the joint (1″ of fabric altogether; see Fig. 10.5). That should leave you with two 53″ strips. Now tack and sew the fabric into sleeves (these should come at the corners) for the spars (Fig. 10.6). Be sure to make the sleeves just large enough to fit the spars snugly. An inch of fabric will make a ⅜″ sleeve. Finally, sew the strips into square loops, making a fourth sleeve where the ends are joined.

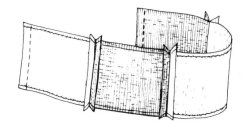

Fig. 10.5. Sewing together the sail covers.

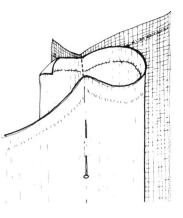

Fig. 10.6. Sewing a sleeve for a spar tube.

Assembling the Kite

Now gather all the parts. Make sure you have the four spars, the three braces, the six half-braces, the three four-hole joints, the twelve one-hole joints, and the two sail covers (Fig. 10.7). Check all measurements.

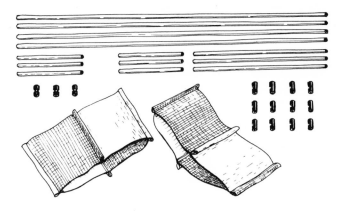
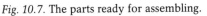

Fig. 10.7. The parts ready for assembling.

When you are satisfied that all the parts have been made correctly, you are ready to assemble the kite. Take one spar and slide a one-hole joint onto it, positioning it exactly in the middle. Now slide a sail-cover sleeve over the spar and then another one-hole joint; slide the other sail cover and another joint on the other side of the center joint (see Fig. 10.8). Now, similarly, slide the center joint, the sail-cover sleeves, and the outer joints onto the other three spars.

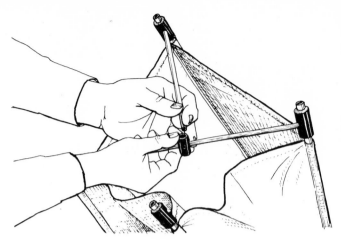

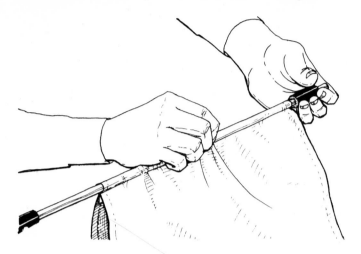

Fig. 10.8. A spar fitted with sail cover and joints.

Position the joints. Now slide the four-hole joints onto the long cross-braces and insert the cross-braces into the spar joints. Up through the next step, the kite will have been saggy and formless. Insert the half-braces. This is the final step and will give shape to the kite (Fig. 10.9). If you find it impossible to fit the half- braces, try trimming them a bit at a time. Also check and if necessary trim the long braces in case they are too long. Do not overtrim, or you will not get the necessary tight fit. Also, trim evenly, so the kite is balanced properly. When you are sure that all dimensions are correct, that all parts are placed correctly, that the braces fit tightly, and that the kite can be assembled and reassembled without difficulty, remove all the braces and dribble just a little resin glue on the spar joints.

Fig. 10.9. Fitting the braces.

The Bridle, Flying Line, and Reel

This kite needs no tail. With just a simple two-leg bridle and metal-ring tow point, it will perform very well. Use about 6′ of cord, pierce the sail covers very carefully, and tie the ends to the spar at the two bridle points (marked with dark circles in Fig. 10.2). Then attach the metal ring. This kite is a really high flier and will withstand strong winds, so use a suitable flying line, and plenty of it. Three-ply heavyweight nylon line carried on a large, well-made reel will do the job.

Flying the High-Tech Box Kite

With a good stiff breeze, the High-Tech Box Kite will really climb. Under the right conditions you can launch it right out of your hands. You may have to adjust the bridle somewhat. Otherwise, you should have no problems. Just make sure to give this kite plenty of room, a good stout reel, and plenty of flying line. It is also a good idea to wear heavy leather gloves to avoid friction burns.